MEMORIES FLOW
IN OUR VEINS

MEMORIES FLOW IN OUR VEINS

Forty Years of Women's Writing From CALYX

CALYX Editorial Collective

Alicia Bublitz, Director
Brenna Crotty, Senior Editor

Editors: Margarita Donnelly, Marjorie Coffey, Emily Eblow, Kryn Freehling-Burton
Beverly McFarlandr>

Editorial Assistants: Diana Oviedo, Kelsey Sutton, Tammy Roebacker, Karen Osovsky

Cover Design: Ryan Brewer, Alexandra Haehnert

CALYX was founded in 1976 by Barbara Baldwin, Margarita Donnelly, Meredith Jenkins,
and Beth McLagan

Memories Flow in Our Veins: Forty Years of Women's Writing From CALYX
© 2016 CALYX, Inc.

ISBN13: [978-1-932010-83-1]

Ooligan Press
Portland State University
Post Office Box 751, Portland, Oregon 97207
503.725.9748
ooligan@ooliganpress.pdx.edu
http://ooligan.pdx.edu

Library of Congress Cataloging-in-Publication Data
[insert CIP data here]

Cover design by Alexandra Haehnert and Ryan Brewer
Interior design by Megan Doyle

[list of text and image permissions if needed. See CMS for conventions]

References to website URLs were accurate at the time of writing. Neither the author nor Ooligan Press is responsible for URLs that have changed or expired since the manuscript was prepared.

Printed in the United States of America

Publisher certification awarded
by Green Press Initiative.
www.greenpressinitiative.org.

This work is dedicated to Margarita Donnelly
daughter, mother, grandmother, dreamer, leader, writer, and force of nature
1942-2014
and
to all the women who have shared their hopes, dreams, pain, joy, and whole selves with us, both on the page and off.

Contents

I BELIEVE I AM BEGINNING

Acknowledgments

Forty years, eighty-six issues of CALYX Journal, over forty books, and countless hours of labor are far too much for a single story. The brief history of CALYX Press and the selections of work presented here are meant to be a mere snapshot of forty years—an enticing slice of a rich, varied, and powerfully activist history. In this project we are indebted to all the authors, volunteers, supporters, readers, and sharers of CALYX over the last four decades. Thank you.

Particular thanks to Beverly McFarland and Marieke Steuben for their compiled histories of CALYX, "A Portrait of CALYX" and "Voices of CALYX: Narratives of Feminist Publishing Activism, 1976-2006" respectively, both of which were used extensively in the development of this manuscript. We encourage readers interested in a deeper understanding of the organization through the years to read these works and consult the CALYX archives at the University of Oregon libraries.

The works presented here are not a "best of" list because, as stated in previous CALYX anthology Florilegia, we do not want women's work to be seen in terms of competition, where one work is placed above another, but rather as a collective expression of women's realities, visions, and dreams. To this end we have arranged the works chronologically and by theme as a means of exploring how women writers have developed common themes in changing ways over our forty-year history.

We hope the remarkable history of CALYX collected here will inspire you to take up the fight for the representation of all voices in publishing: because our work isn't done. Currently, women represent only about one-third of authors published and reviewed in major literary magazines, and women's works are consistently treated as less important, less insightful, less deserving, and just generally less. Read on and make your voices heard.

Alicia Bublitz, Director
CALYX, Inc.

CALYX Defined

Depending on where you look, you'll find that the definition of "CALYX" has a long list of possible meanings that range from the scientific to the mythical to the botanical. These various sources define CALYX as the sepals of a flower, a part of the kidney, a fictional moon, a figure in Greek mythology, or a large synapse in the auditory brainstem structure. Upon finding a spectrum as wide as this, I struggled with the need for a definitive meaning that delineated CALYX's history and the work that we publish here. (I *really* hoped that we hadn't based our journal on "a large synapse in the auditory brainstem structure.")

Eventually, however, I came to the realization that I'm sure many readers have already had; CALYX is, at its core, a well of diverse experiences, mythologies, facts, and perspectives from women all across the country and therefore should not be shackled to one image. CALYX may refer separately to kidneys, space junk, flowers, and gods, in this journal as well in as the dictionary.

So perhaps the best definition of CALYX is the simplest. Coming from the Ancient Greek κάλυξ, it merely means "husk" or "pod," an empty and unexceptional object that is only made remarkable by what is discovered within. We are so grateful to our writers, editors, and readers for filling this husk every year with the beautiful, vital, and astonishing range of art that makes CALYX so varied and unique.

Brenna Crotty, Senior Editor
CALYX Journal

Back in 1975, when Margarita and I were preparing our-selves to launch a "little magazine" of poetry and artwork, my friend Larry Kirkland volunteered many hours of advice and assistance. Larry is a designer who was teach-ing in the Oregon State University art department at the time, and he gave me a crash course on typography and page design, among many other necessary topics. It was Larry who found the image of the poppy that serves as the CALYX logo. One evening in my living room, we began to wonder about a name for the publication as Larry was leafing through the dictionary.

"How about CALYX?" he asked. The definition he read was that of the sepals of a flower, which seemed to us to fit perfectly. In fact, we almost found ourselves inextricably bound to the whole flower motif, but we escaped that trap, thank goodness. Still, the idea of sepals opening to reveal the beauty of women's art and literature, or a husk waiting to be filled with poetry, stories, and painting, seems a fitting way to describe the journal.

That evening was such a long time ago. I am deeply grateful to everyone over the years for keeping the work alive.

Barbara Baldwin, Founding Editor
CALYX Journal

FOR CALYX

Ursula K. LeGuin

—29 September, 1989

CALYX sweet X, crossroads, meetingplace
in the heart of the valley,
CALYX chalice, cup, holygrail
of fierce brightness and fragrance,
CALYX of lazy lilies
full of bees with furry thighs,
vagrants, honey-drunks,
CALYX of fertile words,
holder of the sacred pollen:
on you today this blessing:
 go south in beauty,
 go east in beauty,
 go north in beauty,
 go west in beauty,
 Be in the center in beauty.
 Be a long time in beauty.

THE SPACE WE OCCUPY
Women Embodied

The body. Such an intensely personal thing: a place of self, of desire, of incredible hurt, and of powerful joy. And yet for women, as for so many, this place of birth and of death, of hunger and satiety, of humanity and unspeakable cruelty is never truly our own. Women's bodies have been, and continue to be, possessed, politicized, legislated, and discarded with little thought given to the intersections of place and space through which we move. Even to speak of "women's bodies" simplifies the varying ways in which women inhabit bodies of different color, size, ability, age, location, and nationality.

Throughout history, whenever women look to challenge the status quo, they inevitably are chafing against barriers to their bodies—from the development of Nushu, the "women's language" of the Hunan province in China to ease the physical isolation of foot binding and patrilocal marriage, to the movement for "rational dress" in the nineteenth century West, to ongoing battles over work, family, and reproductive choice. Breaking these barriers by writing freely about sexuality, rape and sexual assault, birth, weight, and aging is an essential part of beginning a dialogue to challenge the cultural notion that women's bodies are mysterious, dangerous, and need to be controlled.

Breaking the taboo of writing about bodies is necessarily compounded by the complicated relationship so many women have with their own—their sexuality, concepts of beauty, and the experience of aging. The reality is that no two bodies are the same; for that reason, many of the pieces shared here may feel intensely personal, but they are also somehow accessible as they become about birth and death, the only universals.

We are taught that great writing is in the head, not the body, that to embody writing is to fill it with shame and mess and complication. Perhaps it would be easier to focus on some Platonic ideal of humanity, rational and infinitely controllable—that which only bleeds when dramatically appropriate, makes love to keep the reader titillated, and exists to be molded to the authorial will. However, rejecting this model breaks authors free to share the focus between the "out there" and the "in here" of our core reaction to ourselves and our experiences—wrinkles and all.

Cinderella Dream at Ten

Ingrid Wendt

1:1 (1976)

Each night under the tree the same wolf
waits for The Beauty to fall
down into the gravel circle the children
draw each day for marbles:

> gravel fine as salt: when it's ground
> into your knees you have to
> let it work itself out.

Each night under the tree the same
wolf waits and no one
is around to save
The Beauty waiting alone inside

her flowing yellow hair with the wolf
snapping at her
plain blue skirts draped gracefully over
the lowest branch

> skirts the mice her only real
> friends will trim with ribbons
> lace scraps her wicked
> step-sisters don't need.

So there's no question: each night you
in your father's car

> (your father driving)

drive past the playground, your heart
in your knees even before

you see her

(in the tree where she always is)

throw open the door, hurry her
into the seat beside
you hurry to slam the door on
the wolf
who is
already gobbling down

(as you knew he would, painlessly)

your legs
from toes
to knees, walking you up right
at the hemline of your own short skirt

knowing it's happened before, knowing your
toes are still there, not to
cry out, knowing

It's after all the price you pay
for Beauty.

Coupled

Barbara Garden Baldwin

1:1 (1976)

They are married. An insect
pinned to the center of her eye,
his image writhes. Swinging open

and shut like the sky
on its hinges she has whittled
stars from his breastbone and placed

them over her sleepless
lids. A rumor spread by the moon,
a ghost who walks electric in her veins

crooning over and over
his name. An incessant rosary.
A handful of rice, whispers and lies.

Her bones hum. A falcon
tied to her prey she stitches
his shadow under her own and rides.

Sorcerer's Apprentice

Barbara Garden Baldwin
1:1 (1976)

You come to life in my hands!
I am the Lady Midas
reclaiming my inheritance.
My touch undoes

the alchemy that froze
your golden bones.
A statue, you live and move
beneath my fingertips.

A charmed serpent, you unwind
inside my veins.
We thrive together, pale lichen
tentacle to bark.

Blue as the skin on a newborn
skull, the pool of
your breath floats in my palm.
We are one.

The idea of anything perfect
begins all over again.

At The Party

Ursula K. Le Guin
Women and Aging (1986)

The women over fifty
are convex from collarbone to crotch,
scarred armor nobly curved.
Their eyes look out from lines
through you, like the eyes of lions.
Unexpectant, unforgiving, calm,
they can eat children.
They eat celery and make smalltalk.
Sometimes when they touch each other's arms
they weep for a moment.

The Idea of Making Love

Alicia Ostriker
Women and Aging (1986)

The idea of making love   as sticking your tongue
into the CALYX of the other   & licking up
its nectar   while being licked oneself   we
love this   because we are always manufacturing
nectar   and when someone sticks a pointy tongue
into us and takes a drop   on the tongue-tip and
swallows it   we make more nectar   we can always
      make more   of our own nectar and
   are always thirsty for the nectar of others

The Crone I Will Become

Jean Hegland
14:3 (1993)

I sometimes think the crone I will become
will miss this blood, this mess, the dear skins
I cradle and soap, these little daughters.
I hoard gifts for her, that wrinkled, dry-
wombed hag, collect trinkets
and pictures, souvenirs
of this fat time. She

hardly cares. Even now I sometimes
glimpse her: Fiercer than any maiden, she stands
unchanging beneath the harvest moon. A black
wind streams her hair, her daughters are grown
and gone, beloved, unnecessary. Her life
is her own, my souvenirs are dead scraps

scuttling in a wilder wind.

Boning

Lorraine Healy
21:1 (2003)

—To Will

At seventeen, he has fallen
flat-on-the-face, out-
for-the-count in love.
The food we buy languishes
in the pantry, dies inside
the fridge. For all we know,
he's surviving on tulips,
or alder pollen. To think,
he says, I used to hate this place...
We shake our heads.
She was born here! This makes
the nettles worthy of worship.

At night, propping the phone
on the bed, he sings her
the country-western songs he
writes for her, the kind
with no heartbreak. Fifteen,
inside her ribcage nestles
a surprising bird from a bluegrass
hill, and fast-moving brooks,
and morning fragrances. This dimpled
marvel, the guile of dew.

So when his far-off friend
asks him, "Are you boning
her yet?", something
hard and edgy hits against
a crystalline place of his,

all of a sudden a gossamer
of cracked glass.

More than two hundred bones
utterly in love with her,
more tissue, white cells, dendrites
than he could count. The marrow
of each bone lit with hunger,
blue with joy. The little spaces
within the marrow of the bones
tunneled by the wild chinooks
of what she brings.

Nobody tells him where biology
and language will collide.
What he knows in his bones today
is his to keep. A man, he chooses
not to grandstand; his steady voice
replies, "No. It's not
like that."

Magnificat

Kirsten Sundberg Lunstrum
20:3 (2007)

Mama says, "The good Lord giveth and He will taketh away." She says this is the taketh—this swollen belly, too big to hide anymore and bursting under my blouse buttons. "God Almighty, child!" Mama screams at me. She screams because I've gone and gave it away—my blessing—my blessing as a woman here on this earth. Mama says girls like me—girls who tell their Woman-secret too soon—tell it not to their husbands in the dark, straight-sheeted beds of their marriages, but girls who tell it like I did—tell it hot and sweaty on afternoons when the sun is fat and dripping yellow down onto everything—girls who tell it for hours on the sticky, vinyl backseats of run-down cars, or loud and long on sweet-faced Joey's squeaky twin bed on Sunday after late Mass—girls like me have names, Mama says. And she says like I don't know. Like I don't know what the thin-lipped, skinny girls down the street whisper when I walk by. Like I don't know that Joey's slicked-back, slack-jawed boys are just waiting for my bubble to pop so they can have a turn. Mama says it like I don't know.

"You look like you swallowed the moon, little girl," my aunty clucks. She and Mama, they sit looking just like a pair, knowing where I'm headed. "And it ain't no place cold," Aunty chides.

I don't care what they know, Aunty all grown and alone, and Mama with three moon-faced babies of her own. Maybe I did swallow the moon. Swallowed it down, slippery as a skinned plum, white and sweet as a tongue. And now it's down there, right inside, full as a new night and bright—so bright. "Yeah," I say back, so mouthy, "I got a glow."

That night with Joey was a full moon night. Big moon,

14   MEMORIES FLOW IN OUR VEINS

blue his face, blue on his dark fingers, on my stomach and in his curly hair. Joey's skin blue and smooth in the moon through the rickrack curtains and the street-out-side-shadows. A full blue moon like a tinfoil candy, and stars cluttered like too many moths. Joey felt like a million moths. Moths under his skin, wings fluttering, batting there just beneath his blue skin.

I wonder if Aunty knows some boys have wings inside them.

Sometimes I see Joey. Joey on the street with his boys and his cigarette-smoke smile, like inside him there's fire. He doesn't say a thing to me—doesn't raise his eyes from the dirt-gutter Hacky Sack game they got going. *That's fine*, I say with words that feel like marbles in my mouth. *I already got him figured inside out*. But when I walk by I see the moth dust still on him—on his skin—and I remember.

"You don't have the time of day for that Joey, or any other crum-bum boys," Mama says, then shakes her head. "I can't believe you! Giving everything away for one sweet day!" Mama tells me she's packing my bags. Sending me to where girls with no sense go—girls who don't make anything of anything but waste. It's a white building with dusty walls and nuns keeping things straight. "I'll pack your bags!" Mama swears ten times a day on Jesus's holy grave.

But so far no bags—no more blue moons, no sense in Mama's cursing moods. Telling the truth, I don't give a damn what Mama says—Mama or Aunty, or that old, forget-me-not Joey. There are things worth the trouble— worth it and wise. Like how his sex feels like a baby mouse, smooth and pink-blue-blind—softer than an old woman's cheek. Like how there's that moment, after, when he's lying there, hair all messed and matted sweaty to his skin, and he looks at you different, like you're not just a girl— not the gangling, pink-faced girl you always think you are. Like for one minute he saw you inside out. And it was so dark and deep and quiet inside that neither of you can say a thing. Secret so big you're left dumb—and almost on your knees. Like he's seen the Holy Mother in there, part of you, and the face of his Mama, and the round tits of Eve, and the fire of just you—all of it you. There's that moment when his lips, bruised purple and licked wet, kiss your skin all up and down in something like a prayer to all the Woman inside you. That's the part that makes my breath come quick, like cold-water drowning or running into the wind. The part that makes me shiver.

Mama shouldn't say it like I don't know, 'cause I do.

She puts her fat hand on the mountain of her hip and says how could I do it? Go out there and just give away the blessing of my purity like it's yesterday's paper—no worth anymore and cheap as life comes? But Mama doesn't get it. She thinks like it's just the fuck—just the rise and crack of bones against bones and the blood-curdle cry of a cunt. She looks at me with brown eyes, fierce as biting dogs, and lashes, "How could you, child, be so sinful?"

At night I rock him, the child in there. I make a picture of him in my head, blue-white and fat-cheeked, sloshing back and forth on my tide, the warm, red waters of my belly. I push my hand against the stretched-tight flesh and think, *maybe that's his head; maybe that's his tiny foot.* And I talk to him, my little one—sing songs that move in the rhythm of his heartbeat, the rhythm of my rocking. And I get that same, breathless, wordless feeling that Mama just can't understand—moon and moth beneath my skin. He's what I know. What I know that Mama and those chick-a-dee girls and Joey's dickless boys could never guess. Say what you want, Mama. I say I'm blessed.

Strong Girls

Donna Miscolta
24:2 (2008)

It was lunchtime and in our corner of the cafeteria, Ofelia and I were on the second of our roast beef sandwiches with extra mayonnaise. Ofelia stopped chewing, though her mouth was still full. Her black eyes bulged and I had just decided to administer the Heimlich when she swallowed. It was loud, like a cork popping. Now looking back, maybe that's what really happened after all. Ofelia popped her cork.

I watched as she headed toward Big Freddy Castillo who had collared one of the scrawny kids who played chess or read Ulysses at lunch. Freddy was actually dangling the kid so that his Redwings danced several inches above the food-littered linoleum.

"Put him down, Freddy," my sister said.

And Freddy did, because now Ofelia offered a more interesting object of ridicule. I wished I'd had a chance to wipe the mayonnaise from her chin, pluck the shred of limp lettuce from her lovely black hair.

"Now which twin are you?" he asked. "The fat one or the fat one?" It was an odd question coming from Big Freddy, who was the only boy in the school almost as big as we were. But rather than engender a comradeship, or even more, a courtship or just a single, no-strings-attached date, our shared physical characteristic only increased the bully in him.

He moved toward Ofelia and her reaction came from a place out of our childhood. She hefted a stocky leg and aimed a cancan kick into Freddy's gut, knocking him off his feet. That might have been the end of it there if she had just walked away. But someone in the crowd yelled, "Go, Ofelia." It was me.

So Ofelia finished the job by throwing her entire weight on the still recumbent Freddy and pinning his shoulders to the floor. As it turned out, Mr. Jarvis, the wrestling coach, was on cafeteria duty that day and he was the one who pulled Ofelia off Freddy and led her away. I followed, expecting him to take her to detention hall, but instead he took her to his office in the gym. He was about to close the door when he saw me and motioned me in too.

We sat down in two sweaty-smelling chairs, and he leaned against his desk, arms crossed, big-knuckled hands wrapped around his biceps.

"You girls ever wrestle?" he asked.

Given our surroundings, we knew it wasn't a metaphysical question.

"No," we said together.

"Builds character," he said, stroking his biceps. "How much you weigh?"

We told him and he nodded. "Come see me tomorrow after school."

That evening after we had polished off the bucket of KFC and the bowl of lettuce our mother had left for us on the dining room table, we mulled over Coach Jarvis's invitation. That's what I called it, as if it were a request for our presence at a social event that required an RSVP.

"I don't think he meant for us to have a choice," Ofelia said.

"Of course we have a choice," I told her.

"Then what's your choice?"

"What's yours?" I asked her back.

"I want to fight," Ofelia said, her broad nose made broader by the flare of her nostrils. "That big oaf Freddy was just the start." Her eyes burned with anger at the Freddys of the world. "I want to win," she said.

I didn't agree with her that Freddy was that big of an oaf, but I realized that I too wanted to win, and I pictured myself in a letterman's jacket, medals pinned at the left breast, a place in the yearbook.

When we were eight, our parents Lyla and Vin divorced and the odd symmetry of two hyper-large proportioned parents was broken.

Though Lyla was our custodial parent, we spent half our time at Vin's, a more stable household, especially after he settled down with his new wife, Vera, a bubble-haired, hoarse-voiced smoker who called us "Doll."

They were managers of an apartment building, and while it was a far cry from the hotel Vin had once hoped to own, they lived rent free and held pool parties every third Thursday. Lyla, on the other hand, who had never quite let go of her ambitions for stardom, first for her and then for us, channeled her energies into a series of entre-preneurial ventures from raising llamas to cactus farming, losing money but never faith, and finally finding her niche selling cosmetics from a vendor cart at the mall.

Our aunts pitied us, our cousins envied us for the lives we led. When we weren't undertaking a new enterprise with Lyla, we were generating tidal waves in Vin's apart-ment pool as we cannonballed from the high dive. We had grown into large and powerful girls with breasts that floated like rafts, a source of envy for our cousins whose thin, underdeveloped bodies fought for buoyancy when we invited them to swim. On one of these occasions, after they had flailed and we had churned in the water for an hour, we spread our towels on the concrete and lay in a circle. There were six of us, three sets of sisters—Rosalie and Julia, Rica and Bonita, and Ofelia and me, Norma.

We talked about our favorite singers and sang Herb Alpert's "This Guy's in Love with You." We talked about being famous one day, and though Bonita insisted she would somehow gain fame as an airline stewardess, I felt in my bones deep within my adipose layers that I would be the one to enjoy renown.

We talked about boys, speculated on which one of us would have a boyfriend first. Rica ruled Rosalie and Julia out with, "Boys don't make passes at girls who wear glasses."

Julia shot back, "Boys don't make passes at girls who are stupid."

"We've been to charm school," Bonita said, sincerely believing that a month of Saturday mornings at the Wendy Ward Academy gave her and Rica the advantage.

None of them considered Ofelia or me as candidates for a boyfriend. But it was something we had talked about privately, the two of us, at night in our twin beds when the lights were out. Ofelia would imagine out loud how a boy, someone bigger and stronger than we were, would place his hands in the vicinity of her waist and pull her toward him so he could press his lips against hers. As I listened, I would slip my hand beneath my nightgown and across the bare skin of my thick thighs and wide hips, the mound of my fleshy stomach, my already balloony breasts. And even if he wasn't bigger and stronger than we were, Big Freddy Castillo appeared behind my closed lids.

But it wasn't until that wrestling season that we first felt a boy's touch. Then we felt it regularly—and in front of large crowds.

We went to the gym, thinking we would humor Coach Jarvis just long enough for him to let Ofelia off the hook for decking Freddy in the cafeteria. But we stayed the whole season, and the gym became our haven and eventually our stage. We met little resistance from the boys on the squad because to them we were a big fat joke. Nevertheless, we were a joke that kicked butt. During practice, Ofelia and I took turns going against Martin Hardcastle, who was the only one in our weight group and the reason Coach Jarvis had recruited us. Martin was like Play-Doh on the mat, and both Ofelia and I perfected our headlock on him. Coach Jarvis, rather than compliment us, bellowed at the struggling Martin, "Do you want to win or lose, Hardcastle?" Martin would wheeze, "Win." But then Ofelia or I, whichever one of us was wrestling him at the time, would slam his shoulders to the mat, expelling from him a loud gasp that surrendered traces of that day's lunch.

Sometimes Freddy slouched in the bleachers, alternately giving his attention to the pert cheerleaders practicing their scissor kicks at one end of the gym and Ofelia and me pummeling Martin at the other end. He emitted low whistles audible enough to make the cheerleaders toss their ponytails in annoyance, audible enough to make Ofelia maintain her hold on Martin a second longer just to make a point, audible enough to make me spring to my feet as gracefully as my size would allow in a pathetic attempt to appear cute and girlish. Soon though Coach Jarvis closed practices to Freddy and all the other looky-loos that came to ogle either the cheerleaders or us. We knew he was frustrated that his plan to use us to build up Martin Hardcastle's repertoire of mental and physical maneuvers was failing. It was true that Martin was getting stronger. But not as strong as we were. He continued to be a pushover. So we practiced on each other, walking through the choreography of a takedown, a reversal, an escape, coaching each other through the moves, eager for our first real opponent.

When we were little—that is, when we were young, Lyla enrolled us in dance lessons. But gravity was our enemy, propelling our round bodies back to the ground almost immediately after we lifted a dimpled knee for a leap or pushed off the ball of a double-E foot for a spin. Lyla developed a squint from scrunching up her face as she watched us, her frown encouraging us back to equilibrium. What she could not squint away, though, were the effects of the leotard, the way the stretchy pink fabric clung to our roundness, bundling at the waist and hips and under the arms.

Strangely, though, we liked our leotards, liked how the elastic captured our body, showed them as they were. And if we couldn't execute leaps and turns in them, we felt a certain compactness of our large bodies that allowed us to move, if not gracefully, at least more powerfully.

Sometimes after dance class Lyla took us to visit one aunt or another. While Lyla and our aunt drank coffee on the front porch, Ofelia and I strutted in our leotards for our skinny cousins who did not take dance lessons. Aunt Millie said her daughters were graceful enough, while Aunt Connie refused to "parade her girls about like poodles."

It was at my aunt Connie's house where Ofelia and I were parading about like poodles that my sister and I got our nicknames one afternoon. We were in the backyard prancing in our Pepto-Bismol leotards for our cousins Rosalie and Julia. We twirled in the patch of crabgrass that was their lawn, our weight pushing our ballet slippers into the bristly blades.

"Do a real dance," demanded Julia who was jealous that we got to take lessons.

Ofelia and I stopped and looked at each other. We thought we *had* been doing a real dance.

Rosalie coaxed us. "Just something easy. Like the cancan."

Ofelia and I retreated to the edge of the crabgrass to talk things over.

"Do we know the cancan?" she asked, no anxiety in her voice, just curiosity.

"Of course," I answered, remaining her of the episode when Lucy Ricardo did it on TV. Sometimes while facing Ofelia, I forgot that she was a replica of me and I saw her as someone wholly apart from me. But then her eyebrow would curve upward the way I knew mine did or she would bite her lip, which was my habit too. That's when I remembered that she was my mirror and I was hers.

"We *can* do the cancan," she said to me. We put our arms around each other's shoulder and strode back toward our cousins. Then in one of those uncannily twin moments, we each lifted opposite legs, kicked each other, and landed on our butts. Our cousins threw themselves down beside us overcome with laughter.

I'm the one who yelped, "Uffy," but Rosalie was already pointing her finger at Ofelia, rechristening her Oafie as she got up to re-enact landing on her cancan. I also performed an encore and now I had a nickname too. "Oafie and Abnorma," Rosalie warbled, and Julia made a chant of it, loud and showy, as they danced around our sprawled and awkward bodies. But Aunt Connie's stinging reproach and Lyla's silent contempt when the back door swung open ensured the ban of the nicknames. Still, they were whispered when we played Red Rover after Sunday dinners, when our skinny cousins would unlink arms to avoid having them broken when Ofelia lumbered toward their line. And they were whispered again after dark when we went inside to play Twister and I lost my balance and splayed across the mat, burying several cousins beneath me.

Oafie and Abnorma. Maybe it should have bothered us more than it did. Instead, we took comfort in our aberration, in the largeness of each other, the space that we occupied, the molecules we displaced when we sat in a chair, stood in an aisle, rode an elevator. There was something about our size and our twinness that made us feel invulnerable. As long as we had each other, we would be fine.

As much as we were reassured by our shared burden, we struggled for selfhood, which is hard to attain when someone is always mistaking you for your sister or her for you. Big Freddy's question to Ofelia as to whether she was "the fat one or the fat one" was the most recent case in point. Being on the wrestling team did nothing to differentiate us from each other. One of us would have to shine. One of us would have to win it all.

One morning we were both in front of the bathroom mirror brushing our teeth. I elbowed Ofelia gently to gain more of the mirror in order to check the job I was doing on my back molars. She elbowed back and I rocked sideways off balance allowing her to insert herself squarely in front of the mirror.

"I was here first," she claimed.

"No, you weren't." I was standing behind her now but peeked around her to see part of me in the mirror. She immediately moved to block my view of myself.

"You don't own it," I said, referring to the mirror, but thinking also of the face that was reflected there.

"Well, I got first dibs." Ofelia stood her ground, ready to swerve left or right to obstruct me from the mirror.

So the competition was on—the first one to the mirror each morning was the first to claim the image there for herself. We took to using all manner of ploys to be the first to the bathroom. One morning as I was quietly crowding my feet into my slippers, Ofelia screamed, "Mouse," and while I jumped onto the bed, testing the springs to the limit, she dashed into the bathroom. Minutes later when she came out, face washed, teeth brushed, hair combed, she was composed, almost smug, and I didn't speak to her until lunchtime when I warned her that if she ate a third sandwich her face would explode from an overdose of mayonnaise.

That night after Ofelia was asleep, I grabbed the alarm clock that sat on the night stand between our beds and buried it under my pillow. If the muffled ringing couldn't wake me, I was sure its vibrations would. But sometime during the night as I wrestled with demons in my dreams, I must have flung the clock onto the floor. When it rang, I vaulted out of bed, startled by the unexpected sound, and collided into Ofelia who had also jumped out of the blocks at the bell. The impact threw us both on the floor with twin thuds against our respective beds where we eyed each other warily, silently measuring the distance to the bathroom door. Our panting was the only sound in the room until Lyla ran in and demanded, "What are you doing?" She had been applying her make-up and only her left eyelashes were glued on.

"Nothing," I answered.

"We fell," Ofelia said.

"Well, be more careful. And quiet." Lyla left to put on the rest of her lashes.

We decided that morning to alternate who had first turn at the bathroom mirror each morning. It didn't matter who woke up first. If I did and it wasn't my turn, I waited for Ofelia to snap out of her stupor. She was a deep sleeper. Ofelia did the same for me. It was not out of consideration that we did this, but a realization that if we didn't, we would hurt each other. The way our parents had.

It's not that Lyla and Vin fought incessantly or loudly or even rancorously. They calmly vexed one another, striking with great accuracy, and then retreating to their separate corners, separate worlds even, leaving Ofelia and me to ours. Sometimes our worlds overlapped. Most of the time they didn't.

Lyla and Vin took us to Disneyland when we were seven, though we looked older due to our size. And by the time Lyla finished dressing us in babyish sailor suit outfits we looked like outlandishly oversized dolls, as much a part of the scenery as the Disney characters that paraded along Main Street or posed in front of the magic castle.

We wore vertical-striped blue-and-white pedal pushers that I suppose Lyla meant to have a slimming effect, but our heavy calves strained the short hem like bulldogs at the leash. Luckily for Lyla, the fashion dictated three-quarter-length sleeves, so our sailor blouses, embroidered with a large blue anchor, covered our thick upper arms and left just our sturdy forearms exposed. It was the sailor hats that Lyla had screwed onto our heads with bobby pins that made us feel conspicuous. She had tilted mine to the left and Ofelia's to the right for a quick way to tell us apart. Otherwise we looked so much alike, Lyla sometimes to take my chin in her hand and angle it this way and that to view my profile—my double chin was plumper than Ofelia's.

"For heaven's sake, Lyla," said Vin, "those hats."

"Vin," was all Lyla said, was all she had to say, her voice throaty like Barbara Stanwyck's in Crime of Passion.

So we walked down Main Street dressed as short pudgy sailors between our two movie-star attractive parents. Lyla wore Audrey Hepburn sunglasses and high-heeled sandals, and Vin wore Troy Donahue sideburns.

Ofelia asked, "Mama, why do people look at us?"

"Because, honey—"

"We're all so doggone beautiful," Vin cut in.

Lyla shushed him as if he'd said something cruel, and she adjusted our hats just so.

It was only after the Alice in Wonderland ride and our reaction to Tweedledee and Tweedledum that we were allowed to ditch the hats. The sight of that paunchy pair in their silly hats made us scream, and Lyla gave in when Vin took us to the hat shop. Ofelia chose Micky Mouse ears and I, in keeping with my second banana status, went for the Donald Duck hat that quacked when its bill was squeezed. It was lost on me that Donald Duck wore a sailor hat.

Now our heads at least blended in with the throngs of

other kids in the park, and we raced for the Dumbo ride. With Ofelia in front and me behind, we filled the cavity of the elephant. As we circled above the crowd, Ofelia operated the lever that raised or lowered our elephant, and each time we passed our parents she brought Dumbo to his base altitude as we tried to wave to them where they sat on a bench below. Lyla, mysterious and unreachable behind her dark glasses, faced one direction and Vin slouched nearby, squinting upward but not at us. When the wind gusted my Donald Duck hat from my head and into the crowd, neither of them saw to rescue it.

Word that our high school had two girl wrestlers got around fast, and at our first match the bleachers groaned under the weight of the curious. Newspaper photographers blinded us with their bulbs as we stretched on the sidelines, and Morocco Smith, the town's hippest DJ, was doing live feeds to the local radio station. Our team had only a small lead when I stepped to the mat, and a hail of cheers and hoots set my ears pounding. I felt a trickle of sweat between my breasts, knew it was darkening the wrestling outfit that was so reminiscent of the leotards that had once put our overflowing proportions on display in dance classes. The elasticity of the suit that contained my largeness made me feel resilient and robust, and I bounced on the balls of my feet as I waited for my opponent—and waited some more, until I realized he refused to come. The referee held my hand up for the victory—but I felt as if I'd been spurned at a dance.

So it was Ofelia's turn, and the boos for my opponent's forfeit turned to wild whoops as her opponent bounded onto the mat like Sylvester Stallone. I understood then that the crowd not only wanted to see the fat girls wrestle, they wanted to see us lose.

The ref blew his whistle, and Ofelia and Sylvester circled each other. In the din of the gym I shouted to Ofelia to let Sly make the first move. Of course she couldn't hear me, but she did it anyway—waited for Sly to lunge at her for a single-leg takedown. She eluded his grab and took advantage of his momentary imbalance with a duck-under, seizing him in a body lock and throwing him to the ground. A singular gasp from the crowd swooshed through the hot gym, ruffled Ofelia's bangs as she sat astride the futile writhings of the boy pinned beneath her.

Ofelia's win made every boy in the league want to put a headlock on us. We were objects of conquest now. So there were no more forfeits, at least not for the next five matches. By that time Ofelia was undefeated and I'd only lost once—to a pervert who blew obscenities in my ear and pinched my nipple on his way to a half nelson. I was disqualified when my heel involuntarily found his testicles.

Parents of the boy wrestlers petitioned the league to banish us from competition claiming we corrupted the sport. When their petition was denied, the forfeits began again. Our muscles clenched, our glands swelled with adrenaline, but with no outlet since with each opponent we faced only rejection.

Morocco Smith called one day and asked to meet with us. At a deli near the radio station, he bought us club sandwiches and fries, and while we chewed, he talked in his smooth DJ voice about our stunning ability, how we were natural audience-pleasers, how we were being cheated, deprived of fans and a venue for our talent. Lyla, who had come as chaperone, beamed *I-told-you-sos* at us, her motherly instincts about our star potential confirmed by this scrawny man who called us "young ladies," as if we were debutantes, though we could have bounced him like a toddler on our knees.

"You deserve better," he told us.

"Absolutely," Lyla said, and we silently agreed.

"I got a plan," he announced, and in the end we went along, not because Morocco promised us a fortune, or Lyla predicted a spread in People Magazine. But because we had so much unspent power, we were willing to use it against each other.

The Battle of the Big Girls was booked at the community college, tickets were sold at TicketMaster outlets, odds were laid. Morocco was already pitching a ten-city tour to promoters. Lyla was shopping for a new outfit. And Ofelia and I were preparing to beat the crap out of each other for a trophy, a title, a little bit of fame.

We hit the weight room twice a day. I spied on Ofelia as she did squats and hammer curls. When I caught her counting my reps on the lat pull-down and bench press, she pretended to be humming.

Though we still looked alike, we didn't recognize each other. Or ourselves. By the time the Battle of the Big Girls was upon us, we had stopped speaking to each other. We ate lunch at separate tables, took separate routes home from school, ignored one another as we settled into our twin beds at night, and tried to be the first to turn out the bedside lamp and leave the other in the dark.

The day before the match I did a light workout—squats and curls and some agility exercises. Then I went to scout out Ofelia who was going a few rounds with Martin. He was no match for her, could no way give her the fight I could. It was a mistake for her to train with him. I knew her moves, her strategies. I knew that I could beat her. I wasn't the only one who knew this.

When I left the gym, I saw Freddy leaning against a pillar near the handball court as if he had been waiting for something. Or someone. My heart had been racing all afternoon in anticipation of the next day, but it quickened even more as I walked past Freddy, intent on snubbing him, playing hard-to-get, maybe. I wasn't sure. But when he called my name, I stopped so suddenly my sneakers made skid marks on the cement.

"Hey, Norma," he said. I turned around and he took a step toward me. Though my palms began to sweat and I regretted not spraying on a little fragrance after my workout, I stood my ground. We'd never really spoken before, and I'd never noticed the details of his face—the slight hook in his nose, the way his eyebrows took too long to taper at his temples. One of his front teeth bent outward a bit, which made his mouth almost sexy, except when he spoke and the wonky tooth seemed to leap out with each syllable.

"My money's on you, Norma."

It hadn't occurred to me before, but of course there would be bets, people taking sides, laying odds.

"Make me a rich man, champ." Freddy punched me lightly on the shoulder. It was gentle, playful. Then he held out a hand for a high-five, and I pressed my palm gingerly to his.

"For sure, Freddy," I said and walked away a little giddy, partly from his touch, partly from guilt. I knew I should have been angry at his motives, but what mattered at that moment was that Freddy believed in me.

We entered the gym from opposite entrances as a band played a gladiator march. Television cameras panned us as we strutted the sidelines, and the crowd stomped and waved. Some high school boys came dressed as us, in long black wigs, their wrestling unitards stuffed with foam breasts. The perky girls from the cheer squad pranced and wiggled in tiny skirts and arced backward in flips or were hoisted in the hands of husky boy cheerleaders. Our skinny cousins munched popcorn in the front row. Beside them sat Lyla who held two bouquets of roses in her lap ready to present to us as if we were contestants in a beauty pageant. "Remember, you're both winners," she had said to us in the car. Vin, who had patted us on the head as if we were large pets, sat with Vera, both of them wearing T-shirts silk-screened with our portraits overlaid with Lucha Libre masks.

It was a spectacle, I thought. But then as I met Ofelia on the mat, the referee between us, I realized we, Ofelia and me, were the spectacle. I looked at her, but I could see it was too late. What was inside of us needed release, and so when the whistle blew, we set upon each other with an aggression that went beyond competition. I took Ofelia down first, but she made a nifty escape and then returned the favor with a gutwrench. But when she followed with a near cradle, she grabbed my top leg, leaving me my bottom one to leverage a breakout. We were both on our feet again, facing each other and the fire I saw in her eyes was the same that I felt burn in my sockets. We were fighting each other because boys could not deal with our strength except by making us demolish each other. "Ofelia," I pleaded. But she lunged at me and I ducked so that in her momentum she soared over me to smack the mat in a slapstick spread-eagle landing. In the laughter that erupted, and amid the hoots and catcalls, I heard the screeching of my cousins as they urged us on. "Go Oafie. Go Abnorma."

We hadn't heard those names since we knocked ourselves on our butts when we were kids. But I took my cue without further prompting. I launched my big body over Ofelia's and did a belly flop on the mat.

Then I raised my butt in the air and pushed off into a forward roll and made a clownish attempt to land in cheerleader splits—a move that spurred the real cheerleaders to toss their pom-poms in appreciation. The hilarity was in full swing as Ofelia, aware now that the competition had turned to farce, happily revived that joke of our youth—the cancan dance. The audience had just begun to clap in rhythm when Ofelia lost her balance. As she stumbled toward me, I put my hand up to break her fall, but her own outstretched hand plowed right past mine, hitting my nose dead center. There was a snapping sensation between my eyes and amid the most penetrating pain as blood poured from my face, down my chest, streaking my leg as it puddled on the mat, I remember feeling a great sense of relief.

In the aftermath, there was no fame or fortune to be had (for us or the Freddys of the world) as a result of our big girl bodies. We declined Morocco's proposal to tour as a comedy team, to make Oafie and Ab¬norma household names. Our bodies would remain ours and so would our names.

A few days later we gathered at Vin's pool with our cousins. We were still minor celebrities and willing to recount the details of our short-lived glory.

"So what was it like wrestling boys?" our cousins in their slinky bikinis asked.

"Anticlimactic," Ofelia said, getting up to climb the ladder to the diving board.

She was right, that in the end, that physical contact with boys, their sweaty bodies against ours, their grip on our flesh, ours on theirs, our eventual pin of their shoulders to the mat—it was nothing, compared to what we had known all along about our strength.

I stretched my wide body across the deck chair, settled some sunglasses gingerly on my swollen nose, and watched Oafie cannonball from the high dive.

CHIEFLY POLITICS, LOWLY GODS

Realities of Injustice

The personal is political—a mantra of a movement, and one made real in the pages of CALYX. While women writing their own stories is an intensely political act, some works are more clearly a critique of culture, exploring the systems that have made us who we are. If we choose to embrace these bodies that are fought over, torn apart, and picked clean by carrion we should also look to the causes of this strife.

The idea behind "the personal is political," that your everyday choices, big and small, have systemic impact far beyond your sphere, has had a powerful impact on late twentieth century and early twenty-first century thinking, but it is also a phrase for a long-recognized problem. Gender, race, sexuality, economic exploitation, colonialism, and globalization are all a part of the ways in which women have experienced the personal, and their political outrage is similarly varied. Temperance supporters singing, "lips that touch liquor will never touch mine" understood that problems at home like poverty and violence were being exacerbated by global economics, advertising, and exploitation of the laboring classes. African American communities understood that a lynching was more than a single death; it was part of a campaign of terror to preserve the status quo. Further tying the exploitation of human bodies as laborers, sexual objects, and casualties of war to the exploitation of the land expands our understanding of the complexity of the human condition.

It stands to reason, however, that if the personal is political, the political is also deeply personal. Just as the global political maneuverings from war rooms have very human consequences, so do the subtler ways in which women and girls learn they are not enough. These selections address the mass atrocities and the micro-aggressions that are a constant and profoundly personal reminder to women that the world is not for us. Some are angry, some funny, and some are certainly both; all give voice to the realities of injustice in powerful ways.

Burning Bride

Chitra Banerjee Divakaruni
Black Candle: Poems About Women from India, Pakistan, and
Bangladesh (1991)

for the victims of dowry deaths in India

1.

In the beginning was fire,
the color of sunrise
through coconut palms,
the color of my wedding *sari*.
Festive with smell of incense
the flames flicked playful tongues.
Stumbling to match his unfamiliar gait
I walked with him
seven times round the fire
while wedding guests threw flowers.

The whisper of fire, secret, enigmatic,
I heard it
under the *brahmins'* rising chants
under the *shehnai* music
flooding our bed like the molten moon.
Fire, too, his eyes, his touch.
His breath a whispered fire. And my sari
spilled on the floor that volcano night
redgashed, a tide of lava.

2.

The day after the wedding
they took off my jewelry, weighed it.
When it came up short

of my father's promise,
they looked at me.
Their eyes glowed pale as coals.

I wrote my father, but I knew already.
The last cow sold,
two sisters left to marry off.
There was no more for my dowry.

They got rid of the servant
who broke coals for the kitchen,
put me to work in that room, windowless,
where slabs lay piled
black on black dust.
Fire in the chest,
each indrawn breath a stabbing flame
as I strained to swing the hammer.

I wrote once more,
again knowing the reply.
If I left my husband's home
the family name would be black,
my sisters left unwed.
I did not write again.

Fire deep in the empty belly,
lying on the dark bedroom floor,
touching my wet face,
not knowing blood from tears.

Had I died,
he could have married again,
a good wife,
one with a dowry.
But though they prayed,
though we all prayed,
I did not die.

3.

I saw them bring the kerosene last night
under the thin crescent
of the failing moon.
They hid the tins
in the women's house, where we spend
the defiled days each month.
They will do it next week
when it is my time,
the dark time of my blood.

I know what happens.
Last month I saw the body
of the night-watchman's new wife.
They gave her a grand funeral,
a hundred guests.

But under the piled jasmines,
the golden sandalpaste,
was the indecent gash of pink,
the skin crisped away,
the smell of charred flesh,
unmistakable,
lodging deep in my belly.
I smell it as I wait.

Did they hold her down, struggling,
oozing the dark oily stain?
Did they silence her cries,
rough hand clamping across lips,
so the only sounds
were the sharp rasp of a match
and the quick blue hiss of fire
leaping in a night turned sudden red?

Killing Color

Charlotte Watson Sherman
Killing Color (1992)

For Beulah Mae Donald, a Black woman who won a $7 million judgment against the Ku Klux Klan for the murder of her son Michael, who in March 1981, at the age of 19 was strangled, fatally beaten, then had his body hung from a tree. Mrs. Donald was awarded the United Klans of Americans, Inc., headquarters property in Tuscaloosa, Alabama. She died September 17, 1988.

They say they got trees over seven hundred years old down in that yella swamp where even the water is murky gold. Bet them trees hold all kind of stories, but ain't none of em like the one I'm gonna tell bout Mavis.

Now, I'm not sayin Mavis is her real name. That's just what I took to callin her after seein them eyes and that fancy dress. Mavis had so much yella in her eyes it was like lookin in the sun when you looked right in em, but a funny kind of sun, more like a ocean of yella fire. You was lookin on some other world when you looked in Mavis' eyes, some other world sides this one.

I first saw Mavis leanin up against that old alabaster statue of some man my Aunt Myrtice call George Washington, but I don't think so cause it's got this plaque at the bottom bout the Spanish-American War and George Washington didn't have nothin to do with no Spanish-American War.

Anyway, I don't like talkin bout that statue too much cause it just gets Aunt Myrtice to fussin and I was always told it ain't right to talk back to old folks, so I don't. I just let her think she right bout things even though I know better. Still, that statue's where I first seen Mavis, and seem like don't nobody know where she come from. We just look up one day and there she was, leanin against that alabaster statue of not-George Washington.

I ain't no fancy woman or what some might call a

  MEMORIES FLOW IN OUR VEINS

hell-raiser, but I know a woman full of fire when I see one, and if somebody hadda struck a match to Mavis, she'da gone up in a puff of smoke.

Mavis got honey-colored skin look like ain't never had nothin rough brush up against her. She had on some kinda blood-red high heel shoes. She the kind wear genuine silk stockins with fancy garters to hold em up, nothin like them old cotton ones I keep up on my leg with a little piece of string tied round my thigh.

Now she was wearin all this right here in Brownville, in the middle of town, in the noonday sun when all you could smell was the heat risin. So naturally I stopped and got me a good look at this woman leanin up against that statue with her eyes lookin straight out at that old magnolia tree front of the courthouse.

Most of us folks in Brownville try our best to look the other way when we walk by that big old barn of a courthouse. In fact, old Thaddeous Fulton, who I likes to call myself keepin company with, won't even walk on the same side of the street as the courthouse, cause most of us know if you brush against the law down here, you sho'nuff gonna get bad luck.

But Mavis was lookin at that old courthouse building full on with them yella eyes of hers never even blinkin, and she did it with her back straight like her spine was made outta some long steel pole.

When Tad come round that evenin, I tried tellin him bout Mavis standin up lookin at the courthouse, but he just shook his head and said, "Sounds like trouble to me." He wouldn't talk bout it no more, which got me kinda mad cause I like to share most of my troubles and all of my joys with this man, and I don't like seein his face closing up on me like he's comin outta some bad story in a book. But that's just what he did when I tried tellin him bout Mavis.

That man had something else on his mind for that evenin. I could tell by the way his eyebrows was archin clear up in his forehead.

Tad's slew-footed as they come and was born with only half his head covered with hair, so the front of his head's always shinin like a Milk Dud. But can't nobody in all of Brownville match that man for kissin.

Seem like he tries gobblin up most of my soul when he puts them sweet lips on his on mine and sneaks his tongue in my mouth. I nearly fell straight on the porch floor the first time he give me one of them kisses, and it wasn't long fore we got started on one of our favorite pastimes—debatin bout fornication. We always waited till Aunt Myrtice dozed off in her settin chair fore we slipped out to the porch and started up our discussion.

"Now, Lady (he likes to call me Lady even though it ain't my given name). Lady, I done lived a good part of my life as a travelin man, and you know I lived in Chicago a good while fore I come back home. And things everywhere else ain't like they is in Brownville. People be different. I knowed quite a few women that was good women. Good, decent women. But we wasn't married or nothin.

We was just two good people tryin to keep they bodies warm in this cold, cold world. Now what's wrong with that?"

"Well, the Good Book say that them livin in the lusts of the flesh is by nature the children of wrath."

"I done seen more of life and people than ever could be put in a book. And I ain't never met nobody that died from lustin with they flesh. What I did see was folks full of wrath cause they wasn't getting no sin."

"Well the Good Book say . . ."

"Lady, I don't b'lieve in no such thing as the Good Book cause I know there's lots of ways of lookin at things and you can't put em all in one book and say this be the Good Book."

"Watch out now, Thaddeous Fulton. You can't come round my house blaspheming."

"I still don't b'lieve in no such book. But I do b'lieve in a good life full of love. Now come on over here and give me a kiss."

Right away I started giggling and actin silly even though I left my girlhood behind fifty years ago. It seems like I never had a chance to be a girl like this and then Tad start up to ticklin me and nobody passin on the road woulda guessed that the muffled snortin lovin sounds was comin from two folks with all kinds of wrinkles all over they bodies.

Tad always ask, "Well, if it's really the Good Book, then shouldn't everything that feel good be in it as a good thing to be doin?"

"That depends on what the good thing is cause everything that feels good ain't good for you," I always say.

"But Lady, look at all the bad that's out there in the world. Folks gotta have some things that make em feel good. Things gotta balance some kinda way, don't they?"

And I always agree there needs to be some kinda balance to what's good and what's bad. Then Tad always starts talkin bout how good he feels just lookin at me and listenin to me talk bout the world.

"I try to show you how much I preciate you with my lips," he say and give me one of them devilish kisses. "Don't that feel good?" he ask and then keep on till we whisperin and kissin and doin pretty near what the Bible calls fornicatin out on the porch.

The next day I went to town and there Mavis was standin in the same spot by that statue, lookin at the courthouse.

Folks was walkin by lookin at her and tryin not to let her see em lookin, but Mavis wasn't payin nobody no mind cause she wasn't studyin nothing but that courthouse and that magnolia tree.

By Sunday, everybody was talkin bout her and wonderin why she kept on standin in the middle of town lookin at the courthouse. Then Reverend Darden started preachin gainst worryin bout other folks's business and not takin care of your own, so I started feelin shamed. But deep inside I was still wonderin bout Mavis. I decided I was gonna walk up to Mavis and found out what she was up to.

Next day, I got up early, went to town, and walked right up and waited for her to say something. But she acted like she didn't even know I was there. So I started talkin bout the weather, bout how that old sun was beatin down on us today, and wasn't it something how the grass stayed green in all this heat? Then I commenced to fannin myself, but Mavis still didn't say a word.

I was standin there fannin for bout five minutes when Mavis turned them yella eyes on me. Now, I heard stories bout people talkin with they eyes and never even openin they mouths, but I never met nobody like that before.

Mavis had them kinda eyes and she put em on me and told me with them eyes that she come for something she lost, then she turned her head back round and fixed her eyes on that courthouse again. Well, it was plain to me she wasn't gonna say no more, and I was ready to go home and sit in some shade anyway, so I did.

That evenin when Tad come by for a visit, he was all in a uproar.

"Why you messin round with that woman?" he ask for I told him I'd stood up at the statue with Mavis for awhile. "I told you that woman sound like trouble. Folks say she rode off with that old Ned Crowell yesterday evenin and he ain't been heard from since."

"Where she at?" I asked. For some strange reason I was scared for her.

"She still standin up there like she always do. Layin back on that old statue. Somethin wrong with that woman. I told you the first time you told me bout her. Somethin wrong. You best stay away from her fore you get tangled up in some mess you be sorry bout. You know how them folks be."

"Don't go and get so upset your blood goes up, Tad. Ain't nothin gonna happen round here."

I tried to make Tad loosen up and grin a little, but he was too worked up and decided he was goin home to rest. I wasn't gonna tell him bout Mavis and her talkin eyes cause he'da probably thought I was losin my mind.

I let three days pass fore I went to town to see if Mavis was still standin at that statue, and sure enough, there she was.

I went and stood next to her and started talkin bout nothin in particular. I fixed my eyes on the courthouse but couldn't see nothin that hadn't been there for at least fifty years.

"You know they keep that building pretty clean and old Wonzell Fitch picks up round the yard every evenin. You might wanna check with him bout findin something you lost," I whispered.

She turned her head and told me with them yella eyes she was lookin for something that b'longed to her. She didn't even hear what I said. I didn't say nothing else, just stood with her for awhile, then went on home.

Tad came by later on with his face all wrinkled up like a prune, but I didn't make fun of him cause I could see he was troubled.

"Seem like three more of them Crowells and one of them Fitzhughs is gone."

"Don't nobody know what happened to em?" I asked. "Don't seem possible four grown men could disappear without a trace. What do folks think is happenin?"

"Don't know for sure, but some folks say they saw least two of them Crowells and old Billy Fitzhugh go off with that crazy woman late in the evenin."

"Do the sheriff know bout that?" I asked.

"Naw, and ain't nobody gonna tell him neither. If they do they likely to get locked up."

"Well, sure is mighty strange. Didn't think she even left that spot at the statue to go relieve herself. She just stand there starin, don't ever see her drink no water or nothin, just standin in all that heat."

"Well, look like come evenin she find herself one of them old white men and go off with em and don't nobody see that man no more. You ain't goin round her, is you? I sure hate to see what happen when the sheriff find out bout her being the last one seen with them missin men, cause you know well as I do what that mean."

Me and Tad just sat together real quiet and still on the porch holding hands like old folks is supposed to do.

Next day I had to take Aunt Myrtice to evenin prayer service so I decided I was gonna sit outside and watch the statue from the front steps of the church.

"You bout to miss service and then have the nerve to sit on the front steps of Reverend Darden's church?" she fussed.

"I'm gonna do just that and ain't nobody gonna stop me, neither."

"You gonna sit outside when you need to be inside?"

"Yep," I replied. Then I just stopped listenin. I already made up my mind bout what I was gonna do, and even Aunt Myrtice's fussin wasn't gonna change that.

So after all the folks had gone inside, I sat on the porch and watched the sun go down and watched Mavis standin at the statue looking at that same building she'd been lookin at for almost a month now.

When the shadows had stretched and twisted into night, I saw the lights from some kinda car stop in front of the statue. Mavis jumped in the car with what sounded to me like a laugh, and the car eased on down the street.

"No tellin where they goin," I thought out loud as the car moved slowly past the church. I could see the pale face of old Doc Adams at the wheel. Mavis never even turned her head in my direction or anyone else's. Her yella eyes was lookin straight ahead.

"Nuther man gone," Tad mumbled when he stopped by the next day.

"Was it old Doc Adams?" I asked, scared to hear the answer.

"How'd you know? I done told you you better stay way from that woman. God knows what she's up to and I sure don't want no parts of it. You askin for trouble, Lady, foolin round that woman. Best go on in the house and read some of that Good Book you always talkin bout. I know it don't say nothin good bout killin folks!"

"Now how you know anybody been killed, Tad? How you know that? Some folks is just missin, right? Don't nobody know where they at, right?"

"You don't have to be no schoolteacher to see what's happenin! Them men be dead. Just as sure as we sittin here, they dead! Now you better stick round home with Miss Myrtice cause this town gonna turn upside down when they go after that woman!"

That night I turned over in my mind what Tad had said. Could Mavis have killed all them men? How could she do it? She ain't even a big woman. How could she kill even one grown man, even if he was old? And why wasn't the sheriff doin something bout it? Couldn't he see Mavis standin right in the middle of town leanin on that statue, like we see her every day?

I could feel pressure building up in my stomach, a kinda tight boilin feelin I always got when something big was bout to happen. So I decided I best go up to town and tell Mavis to be careful cause folks was sayin and thinkin some pretty nasty things bout her. Not cause of the way she was dressed, but cause of her bein seen ridin off with all them white men and ain't nobody seen em since.

Well, there she was standin in her usual spot with her eyes burnin holes in the courthouse. I didn't have time to mince words, so I didn't.

"Folks is talkin, Mavis. Talkin read bad bout you. Sayin crazy things like you tied up with the missin of some men round here and how you up to no good here in Brownville."

Mavis didn't say a word, just kept on lookin.

"This town'll surprise you. You might be thinkin we ain't nothin but backwoods, country-talkin folks, but we got as much sense as anybody else walkin round on two legs. And don't too many people sit up and talk this bad bout somebody they'd never even laid eyes on a month ago without some kinda reason and some pretty strong thinkin on it. Now I don't wanna meddle in your business none, but I think you got a right to know folks is callin you a murderer."

Mavis turned them yella eyes on me for so long I thought I might start smoking and catch afire. I mean, she burned me with them eyes: "I come for what is mine, something that belong to me, and don't none of y'all got a right to get in my way."

I stepped back from her cause she was lookin pretty fierce with them eyes of hers alight, but I still reached out to touch her arm.

"I just hate to see bad things happen to folks is all. I don't mean no harm."

And I turned to walk away. But it felt like a steel band grabbed my arm and turned me back round to look at them yella eyes: "Now you listen, listen real good cause I want all of y'all to know why I was here after I'm gone and I'm not leavin till my work is done.

"Way back when, I lived on what was called Old Robinson Road. Wasn't much to look at, but we had us a little place, a little land, some chickens and hogs. We growed most of our own food right there on our land and didn't hafta go off sellin ourselves to nobody. Not nobody, you hear me? We was free people: livin our lives, not botherin nobody, not messin in nobody's business, didn't even leave the place to go to church. We just lived on our land and was happy.

"Now some folks right here in this town got the notion in they heads that colored folk don't need to be livin on they own land, specially if it was land any white man wanted.

"Old Andy Crowell, who looks like the devil musta spit him out, got it in his head he was gonna take our land. Well, I don't know if they still makin men like they made mine, but my man knew and I knew wasn't nobody gonna get this land, not while we was standin and drawn breath.

"So we took to sleepin with a shotgun next to the bed and one by the front door, and my man even carried a little gun in his belt when he was out in the fields. I kept one strapped to my leg up under my dress.

"We went into the courthouse right here, and tried to find out bout the law, cause we knew had to be a law to protect us, one for the protection of colored folks seein as how slavery had been over and wasn't no more slaves we knew bout.

"We went up to that building and s'plained to a man what call hisself a clerk that we had a paper tellin us to clear off our land. My man had the deed to that land cause he got it from his daddy who got it some kinda way durin slavery time, and nobody bothered him bout it cause he didn't let nobody know he had it.

"But it was his and we had the paper to show, and that ratfaced gopher callin hisself a clerk looked at the deed to our land—our land I'm tellin you—and that clerk took the deed to our land and crumbled it up and threw it on the floor and told us to get outta his office.

"My man was just lookin right in that clerk's face. Wasn't flinchin. Wasn't blinkin. Just lookin. But his eyes, oh his eyes was tellin that man a story, a story that old fool didn't even know he knew. And my man told that clerk all about it, and I picked up the deed to our land and we left.

"Well, it wasn't long after we'd gone to the courthouse

fore they come for him.

"You know how they do.

"Sit up and drink a buncha liquor to give em guts they don't have, then they posse up and come ridin for you soon as the sun go down.

"You know who it is when you hear all them horses on the road. Then you look through the window and see them little flickers of light comin closer and closer, growin bigger and bigger till it looks like the sun's come gallopin down the road. They they all in your yard holdin up they torches till the yard's lit up like daylight, you know it's the devil's own night. You can smell him out in the yard all tangled up with flint and sweat and liquor. I know the stink of evil anywhere. Then my man picks up his gun and steps out into that red night and tells em to get off his land or he'll shoot. I could see the claws of the devil pullin on my man and I tried to pull him back to the house, but he pushed me back inside and his eyes told me how he loved me like he did his own life. Then the devil's fingers snatched him and his tongue wrapped round my man's arms and drug him out into the middle of satan's circle, where they all had white handkerchiefs knotted round they faces from they red eyes to they pointed chins.

Then they knocked my man down with his own shotgun and they kicked him, each one takin a turn. I picked up the shotgun standin near our bed and ran out the house screamin and fired a shot. Two of em fell to the ground, but some of em grabbed me from behind and beat me in the head. By the time I opened my eyes, my man was gone. It was Edith Rattray who come round and found me lyin in the yard and cleaned me up and nursed me. I musta laid in bed for over a month fore I could get up and go to town and find out what happened to my man.

"And what I found out was this: Evil can grow up outta the ground just like a tree filled with bad sap and turn every livin thing to something rottin in the sun like an old carcass.

"Now, you tell them folks what's wonderin why I'm here and what I'm doin and what I'm up to, you tell em that I'm cleanin that tree right down to the root."

Sayin that seemed to make that cold steel band slip from my arm. Mavis turned her eyes back on the courthouse.

~)

I sat on the porch even though it was the middle of the noonday sun and thought about what Mavis' eyes had told me.

"I must be losin my mind," I said to the listenin trees.

How in the world could a woman tell me any kinda story with no sound comin outta her mouth? What kinda woman was she? And what kinda woman am I? And what would God say bout all of this? I went inside the house and reached for my Bible. Surely some kind of answer could be found there.

After readin a while, I still hadn't found the answer I was lookin for, so I went into the kitchen and started cookin instead.

"What's for supper, daughter?" Aunt Myrtice asked.

"Oh, I'm fixin some squash, some fried catfish, some salt pork, a pot of blackeye peas, a pan of cornbread, and some peach cobbler for dessert."

"Um um. Tad must be comin by. I know you ain't fixin all that food for just me and you."

"Yeah, Tad did say he was comin round here later this evenin. Maybe I'll take you up to prayer meetin fore he gets here."

"Umhum. Y'all gonna get me outta the way so you can sit in this house kissin while I'm gone. You oughtta be shamed of yourself, old as you is."

"I might be getting on in years, Aunt Myrtice, but I ain't dead yet." I kept on cookin.

I decided I was gonna get Tad to help me watch and see

what Mavis was up to that evenin after we dropped Aunt Myrtice off at the church.

"You want me to do what?" Tad shouted after I told him what I wanted. "I ain't goin nowhere near that woman and you ain't either. You wanna get us both killed?"

I patted his arm and talked to him soft as I could to try to calm him down. No sense in his blood goin up over this foolishness.

"Tad, I just wanna prove to you and everybody else that Mavis ain't killed nobody and she ain't done none of us no harm by standin up by that statue. She can't even talk, how she gonna killa big, old man?"

Tad gave in even though I could see he didn't wanna. He parked the car bout a block away from the statue. We didn't worry bout whether or not Mavis could see us cause she wasn't lookin at nothin else but that tree in front of the courthouse.

"Now look at her. You know something wrong," Tad said.

"Don't go and start workin yourself up. We ain't gonna be here long cause it's already startin to get dark and you said she usually leaves bout this time, didn't you?"

"I don't know when she leaves, cause I ain't been round here to see it. Folks just been sayin she leaves bout this time."

"Well, we'll wait a little while and see."

Sure enough, fore too long, an old red pickup pulled up next to Mavis and she ran around the front of the truck and jumped inside.

Even from where we was parked we could hear the sound she made when she got in the car. It wasn't no laugh, like Tad said, it was more like a high-pitched cryin sound mixed up with a whoop and a holler. It made the hair on the back of my neck stand straight up, and Tad said it made his flesh crawl.

Anyway, the truck pulled off and we followed a ways behind it. Couldn't see who was drivin on accounta that big old rebel flag hangin up in the back window.

We followed em anyway: out past the old poorhouse, past the pea and okra shed, past the old Lee plantation, out past Old Robinson Road.

Tad started getting mad again cause he wanted to turn round and go back home. "You know we goin too far from home. Ain't no tellin where that crazy woman goin."

"Hush, and keep drivin. We gonna prove something once and for all tonight. Put a end to all this talk bout murder."

So we kept on drivin, but it was so dark now, we couldn't really make out what we was passin.

After a while, Tad said, "I don't think we in Brownville no more. You can tell by the shape things make in the dark."

I didn't say nothin. Just kept my eyes on the truck's red lights in front of us. A few minutes later, the truck pulled off the road and went into the trees. When we reached the spot where they turned off, we couldn't see no road, no lights, no nothin. Just trees.

"Well, I guess this is far as we go. Ain't nowhere to go now but back home," Tad said. "They probably went back up in them woods to do they dirty business."

"What dirty business, Tad? What dirty business? First you callin her a murderer, now what you callin her?"

"What kinda woman drive off with men in trucks in the evenin? What you think I'm callin her?"

"Let's just walk a ways in there to see if we can hear something."

"I'm not walkin back up in them woods. Now you go on and walk up in there if you want to, I ain't goin nowhere but back home."

While we was fussin, a car pulled off the road next to Tad's car. A skinny-faced man leaned out the window.

"You folks havin trouble?" he asked.

"I musta made a wrong turn somewhere back down the road and we just tryin to figure out the best way to get back home," Tad replied.

"You sure musta made a wrong turn cause ain't nothin out this way but trees and swamp."

"Is that right?" Tad asked.

"Yep, that's right. That big old yella swamp is bout two miles in them trees and it ain't nowhere no human man or woman needs to go. Ain't nothin livin that went in that swamp ever come back out that way. Nothin but the shadows of death back up in there. You step through them trees and it's like you stepped down into a tunnel goin way down into the ground. Down there them old snakes hangin down from them trees like moss is yella. Mosquito bites turn a man's blood yella. Yella flies crawl on the ground where worms come up out the yella mud and twist like broken fingers from a hand. Shadows come up and wrap they arms round you, pullin you down into yella mud where sounds don't come from this world. Nothin down there but yella."

Me and Tad thanked the man and turned the car around and went back home. The skinny-faced man's word burned our ears.

"Now don't you try to get me to run round on no wild goose chase behind that woman no more. I don't care what she's up to, I don't want nothin else to do with her."

Next day first thing, I went to town to talk to Mavis. Sure enough, there she was standin next to that statue.

"I been thinkin bout what you told me bout the evil way back when, and it seem it might be better just to let things lay and forgive the ones that did it like Jesus would."

Well, what did I go and say that for? Mavis whipped her head round and shook me with them eyes.

"Who you to forgive all that blood? Who YOU? Put your head to the ground and listen. Down there's an underground river runnin straight through this town, an underground river of blood runnin straight through. Just listen."

Then her eyes let me go and she turned back round.

When I turned to walk back home, I saw some old dried-up mud caked round the bottom of that red dress she was wearin, mud that was yella as mustard, but dried up like old blood.

Not long after Mavis shook me up with them yella eyes of hers, I got sick and Aunt Myrtice, poor thing, had to tend me best she could, bless her heart.

Tad came by and helped when he could, but I'm the type of person don't like folks to see me hurtin and I sure didn't want Tad to keep seein me with my teeth out and my hair all over my head, though he claims I still look good to him.

Aunt Myrtice act like she don't hear him, but I could see her eyes light up.

Once I got to feelin better and was almost back on my feet, Tad started hunchin up his eyebrows, so I knew pretty soon we was gonna go out on the porch and get to arguing bout fornicatin, which to tell the truth, I'd rather be fussin over than that foolishness bout Mavis.

But Tad told me Mavis wasn't standin up at the statue of not-George Washington no more and nobody knows where she went off to. She just disappeared easy as she come.

The sheriff never did find out bout her. It turned out all them old missin men had been tangled up with the Ku Klux years back and had split plenty blood in the yard of that courthouse, hangin folks from that magnolia tree.

Sometimes, now, I think bout what Mavis told me how evil grow up outta the ground and how that old underground river flows with blood, and I think about putting my head to the ground just so's I can listen. But I just go and stand by that statue and look up at that courthouse, feelin Mavis in my eyes.

Waikīkī

Haunani-Kay Trask
Light in the Crevice Never Seen, (1994)

all those 5 gallon
toilets   flushing
away tourist waste
into our waters

Waikīkī   home
of *ali'i*
sewer center
of Hawai'i

8 billion dollar
beach   secret
rendezvous for
pimps

Hong Kong hoodlums
Japanese capitalists
haole punkers

condo units
of disease
drug traffic
child porn

AIDS   herpes
old fashioned
syphilis
gangland murder

gifts of industrial
culture for primitive

island people
in need

of uplift   discipline
complexity sense
of a larger world
beyond

their careful *taro*
gardens   chiefly
politics, lowly
gods

Waikīkī: exemplar
of Western ingenuity
standing guard against

the sex life
of savages

the onslaught of barbarians

Why a Woman Can't Be Pope

Sandra Kohler
16:1 (1995)

Everyone knows that under her robes,
there would be breasts,
the nipples brown raspberries,
a sloping mound, furred,
the cleft in the fur where
a tongue fits, furled layers,
lips, between them the tunnel
into the last world.

Melissa Is My Name

Mary Beth Deline
16:3 (1996)

So you work at McSomethings.
Slave labour. Cheap teeth.
And the manager says
      "Please make it brief"
says to close up again
"You don't mind
do you"
& you consider stabbing him
with your name tag pin
jab i am not wendy jab i am not wendy jab
i am melissa melissa melissa is my name.
& you step into the black
licorice suck of the parking lot.
fingers grabbing pulling cheap polyester
ripping off your hat,
braids curling out shy underneath
as the slam is softened
and they breathe
"She's a girl" & you are born
into the arms
of the two cops
stuttering sweating sorry sorry sorry.
"We didn't know you were a girl"
& you think how you work all day at school

The Rash

Sue Pace

19:2 (2000)

My father was a quiet man—restrained in speech and personal habits—who preferred reading in the den to almost any other activity, including kissing his children good night. At least that's how it appeared to us, the three children in question. Our mother reassured us constantly that he loved us and that he was proud of our various accomplishments. "Your father is the kind of person who doesn't express himself easily," she would explain. By that she meant he was unlike herself, who expressed herself continually to whoever would listen.

It wasn't that he ignored us completely. He watched my violin recitals and my sister's sporting events but in silence. My brother, Dan, was neither athletic nor artistic but was on the debate team and on the staff of the student newspaper. In high school he became a rabid Christian, in college a liberal atheist pro-abortionist, and is now a trial attorney for a conservative law firm. I think it's been difficult for a man like my father—a man who prefers to move through life like water—to under stand my brother's intense opinions and argumentative ways.

Nevertheless, Dan confided to my sister and me (before this year's dismal Christmas as we adult children shivered in the driveway, preparing to enter our ancestral home) that he never felt so close to our father as when they were arguing in terse spurts about gun control, gay rights, or immigration. "I really don't give a fuck one way or the other," Dan said. "I just take whatever side he's not on." I then spoke of the intense jealousy I felt when I saw Father clench his hands into fists and rise from his seat to yell hoarsely when my sister, Lydia, made her first varsity fast pitch home run.

In an act of uncharacteristic generosity, Lydia assured me Father had actually groaned when told (by our mother, of course) that I had missed the trill at the end of a cascading line of arpeggios during violin auditions for the Junior Symphony.

"I heard it, Allene," Lydia said. "He groaned."

We trooped into the house and later (Father was in the kitchen making coffee) Dan mentioned it again, a bemused expression on his face. He couldn't imagine groaning over a missed trill. I could though, and my face burned with shame for that fractured event. I am the oldest, can't you tell?

As we all sipped coffee—Dan had promised his fiancée, Serene, to control his alcohol intake over the holidays—we began the recollection of older, more comfortable stories. Stories with Mother at the center. It was she who both warmed us and scorched us. She bustled and bristled and took us to the zoo, to the theater, and later taught us to drive. She paid our allowances and yelled at us when we came home late with dilated pupils and beer or worse on our breath.

But this story is about our father, a man extravagant only in the amount of wiry brown hair sprouting from his shirt collar and cuffs. Dan called him The Hirsute One all through high school and still would except for Mother's intervention. Father was an English instructor at Lakecrest High—the snooty private school for the bright and wealthy—and when he wasn't reading or correcting adolescent sestinas, he was ghosting Nancy Drew mysteries. While I was at Cornish Art School, I asked Father why he didn't write real fiction instead of canned mysteries for simple-headed junior high girls. I was quite full of myself back then, having just recognized my homosexuality, and even though I couldn't quite come out to my family, I was anxious to show my independence from them. I had no lover but I had plenty of angst, which I perversely took out on my father. "Why write something so predictable?"

I asked. "I mean, this isn't art you're writing, it's drivel."

To my surprise, he didn't take offense. Instead he filled an entire Sunday dinner with the challenges of writing to spec. "The formula is very confining and that's what makes it so interesting. The first chapter has to introduce Nancy. I have to include her background and show what she looks like and how she dresses and moves. I like to add dialogue right away so that any girl who's read all 118 books in the series won't be bored at the beginning. Chapter two is to set up the problem and introduce new characters. Chapter three . . ."

Father droned on through twenty-seven chapters—scene, exposition, dialogue, rising action, climax, resolution. Mother yawned, Lydia scowled, and Dan filled his plate three times with meat loaf and mashed potatoes. I watched the way Father's eyes glowed and how his hands moved. I wanted him to look at me, to talk about me, with the same intensity that he talked about Nancy Drew.

That was while I was in college. Earlier, before I passed through the horror of adolescence, I had learned to never bring friends home after school for fear of finding my father in one-inch pumps and a straight skirt and climbing from table to chair to see if Nancy could jump between box cars or scramble up the cliffs above the imaginary town in which she lived. Most often, though, he was spread over the couch like a frayed and folded afghan, outlining plots and dropping crushed balls of notebook paper onto the rug beside him like shriveled fruit.

His relationship with Mother was a subject rarely of interest to me. Not until after she left him did I pick at it in the empty moments of the present—stuck in traffic, for example, or waiting for my lover to put away her bassoon and come to bed.

The fall and winter after Mother left him, our house on Queen Anne Hill became noticeably darker. Not only because Father's inherent stinginess was allowed free rein without Mother's moderating excesses, but because his life shrank to conform to his single state. The kitchen, the bedroom, and the bathroom lights winked on and off depending upon his physical needs. Once a week I would enter through the back door and climb to the master bedroom at the top of the stairs. There—fully dressed but wrapped in the bedspread—he was usually curled on the queen-sized bed. Books were stacked thigh high while the television blared whatever buy was available on the shopper's channel.

"Jesus, Dad, can you turn it down a little?"

He fiddled with the remote control, dropping the volume infinitesimally, and placed the thin book of poetry he was reading face down on the rumpled sheets, where it resembled an illustrated moth. His voice was raspy and pinched and I couldn't understand his words.

"What?" I asked. "Your what?"

He flicked the remote and the screen went blessedly blank. "I said my rash is worse."

Mother's stated reason for getting an apartment in the University District was to work on a series of related one acts. She hoped to use them as her doctoral dissertation. Her TA stipend was for three quarters. Over Labor Day weekend she informed us all (including Serene, who was doing the perfect fiancée bit by cleaning the barbecue grill) that she wasn't keen on settling in New York or LA But Minneapolis was a good theater town and so was Houston. It all depended upon how her dissertation went. She planned to be a dramaturge. She hoped we understood it was time for her to get on with her own life now that we were all settled. Mother's words were bright as lasers dancing in the night.

In my memory Father's rash erupted almost immediately after her announcement. Dan, however, remembers the complaints developing slowly over Christmas—by then Mother had been gone an entire quarter and was spending winter break with colleagues skiing on Crystal Mountain while we (her family) gathered in the old house and ate deli turkey and frozen pumpkin pie on double-thick paper plates. Lydia (who was getting an MSW and doing research for the Public Health Department on the sex lives of the homeless in San Francisco) wasn't convinced there ever was a rash. Lydia hasn't been back to Seattle since Christmas and is, you must understand, the one most like my mother. She has little sympathy for a father who does nothing except bitch about the condition of his skin. Her words, not mine.

So there is no agreement among us. I, always the peacemaker, call my mother. "His rash is worse."

"And how are you, Allene?" Mother croons. "Are you still composing? Where is the symphony touring this year?"

"It's definitely worse," I insist. "I've seen it."

Mother sighs, either exasperated or resigned. I am almost as bad as my father at reading her moods and deciphering what she truly means. "Has he seen Dr. Latham?" Mother's tone is, I decide, reluctant.

"Latham retired."

"Oh, that's right. Well, has Lee gone to anyone?"

I close my eyes and see her face—vibrant and alive—with freckles, short red hair going gray, and the amber eyes of a cat. I want her to call this man his proper title. My father. She insists on calling him Lee.

"He hates change," I say. "You know how he hates change."

"He's fifty-seven years old and if Lee has a rash he can certainly rouse himself to make a doctor's appointment."

I am sullen. "That's what you would do."

"It's what any rational person would do."

I try another tack. "He's depressed. It's very difficult for someone who's depressed to dig his way out. It takes a great deal of energy and support from other people."

"Stop projecting your own anxieties. Lee is not depressed. He is taking stock, yes, but he is not depressed."

I'm painting a bad picture of my mother. The words on the page do not show her sense of style. Her vibrancy and the humor with which she speaks don't come through. Mother isn't wicked or cruel or sarcastic. She simply doesn't see the magnitude of the problem.

"You don't understand." The desperation in my voice is embarrassing. "You've never been depressed."

"Of course I have."

"You haven't," I continue doggedly. "You soldier on through life, you and Lydia, and can't even begin to comprehend how debilitating depression can be."

"I understand." A slight edge has crept into her tone.

"You don't!" I scream into the phone—something I've never been able to do to her face—and slam down the receiver.

I email Dan. The words flow from my fingers quickly and I send it, mistakes and all.

> She refuses to listen .Why won't she eventry to understand? Can't she see wha't happeningto-him/ She just can't ABANDON HIM THIS WAY . hE HAS this horrible rash. He's your father, DAn. At least call him! !

While I am emailing Dan, my mother is emailing me.

> I KNOW YOU THINK I AM A HEARTLESS BITCH BUT PLEASE, TRY TO SEE MY SIDE OF IT. YOUR FATHER DOESN'T NEED YOUR PROTECTION, ALLENE. HE NEEDS TO EMBRACE HIS OWN LIFE. LET HIM GO. THAT'S WHAT LOVE IS ALL ABOUT.

There is more. A veritable warehouse of dangling prepositions, plus the usual pronouncements of affection and a short paragraph defending her claim to be a familiar of depression, all of it in capital letters.

> ASK YOUR FATHER IF YOU DON'T BELIEVE ME, is her parting shot. I WAS IN THE THROES OF

POSTPARTUM DEPRESSION FOR A YEAR AFTER
YOU WRER BORN.

I email Lydia (the baby of the family) a message similar
to the one I sent Dan. I have calmed down enough to
check for spelling, typos, and punctuation. I forward it
with Mother's note intact. Lydia emails back the next day.

Allene, I'm in the middle of midterms. Don't send me
any more stupid messages.

P.S. I can't find my passport. Would you check to see if
it's still at home or try the family safety deposit box–and
FedEx it to me. I need it to sign up for work-study in
Mexico City. Gracias.

I have overcome the failed trill and play third violin in the
Seattle Symphony. We are preparing the spring program
but between twice-daily rehearsals I stop by the house. I use
my key to get in and catch my father in the kitchen with
his pants down. Literally. His briefs are silky and his belly
is no longer paunchy. He has, in fact, the look of someone
who resides in a concentration camp. Every hair on his
body has disappeared. Also the hair on his arms and legs
is gone. There is a light dusting of red over his shoulders
and down his arms. I wonder briefly about leukemia and
then about male anorexia (not unheard of) and try twice
before any words actually come out of my mouth.

"Where's your robe, Dad?"

"I wasn't expecting company. What are you doing here?"

"Lydia needs her passport. Is it here?"

He grunts and continues guarding the toaster. The
second the toast is ejected, he butters it and eats at the
counter, standing up. Crumbs are everywhere along with
empty soup cans and unopened packages of Fig Newtons.
My father is—used to be—a modest person. I had never

seen him in bathing trunks without a tee shirt and now I am seeing him in silk underwear. I do not know where to look. The countertop holds a dozen brown bottles of vitamin pills and cardboard cans of supplemental powders. I try to remember if I noticed hair sprouting from his collar over Christmas. I try to remember if his knuckles were bare then too.

"Listen, Dad? Lydia thinks it's here? Or we could try the safety deposit box?" I've begun forming declarative sentences as questions. It is a sign of stress.

He dips a rectangle of toast into the bowl of applesauce at his elbow. It is comfort food for him. I watch him poke half a slice into his mouth and chew thoughtfully.

"Do you know where her passport is?" I repeat. "Have you seen it lately?"

"No." He finishes off another slice of toast before he speaks again. "Did I tell you I have a rash?"

"You told me."

"It's worse." He holds out a smooth arm and I nod sagely.

"You should see a doctor."

"It might be in your mother's old jewelry box," he mutters, "or you could try the desk in the den. Top right drawer."

I climb the stairs to my parents' bedroom and pick through the jewelry Mother didn't take with her into her new life. The pearl earrings and necklace Serene will eventually get are there, along with a jade bracelet that will probably go to Lydia and an opal ring that will, no doubt, belong to me after Mother dies. Which will be in thirty or forty years, as her side of the family lives forever. My father's family dies on the dot at seventy-three. All of them. The DNA self-destructs and that's the end of it. No lingering. No early warning system. They get a heart attack or a stroke and die. Every single one.

I do the math as I do it every week. Fifty-seven from seventy-three. Father has sixteen more years to go. Does he know that I am lesbian? Would he care? Would he want to meet my lover? Should I fake it—my life—until he dies?

There isn't much else of value in the jewelry box. Some fluorescent earrings from the seventies. Some hand-strung bead necklaces from the early nineties. Little Ziploc packages filled with baby teeth from Dan, Lydia, and me. I am enraged at the sight of those labeled plastic envelopes. How could Mother abandon those mementos? How could she walk out on my father—my past—that way?

He wanders into the bedroom. "Here it is."

"Where did you find it?"

"With the bills."

I flip open the passport. The photograph inside could be Mother when she was twenty-three, with surging red curls and rosy cheeks. But it is Lydia between the green covers, glowing with health and determination. I tuck the slim booklet into my purse. My father's blue eyes brim with something: Tears? Eye drops? Smoke from the toaster? I do not know how to enter uncharted territory. I strive for a light touch.

"Any shut-off notices lately?"

He shrugs. "Most of the payments are taken directly out of the account."

"So you aren't writing checks these days."

"A few. I haven't gotten the hang of debit cards. It's hard to keep track of things."

"How are classes?" I have never asked him about classes before but his sudden tears and pale smooth body unnerve me. "How are those old midterms going?"

"Didn't I tell you?" He raises an eyebrow. "I'm on sabbatical."

"When did that happen?" I keep my voice steady but he will notice the pinched quality. It will speak volumes.

"In September."

I realize with an almost physical jab that he hasn't been working since Mother left and none of us knew. None of us.

I occupy myself with the clasp on my purse. It is a long minute before I can speak. "When are you going back? To work, I mean?"

"It's hard to say."

He scuffs out of the bedroom, flicking off the light as he goes, leaving me in layers of shadow. The symbolism is almost perfect, except my personal darkness is far blacker than the golden light of a setting sun that strains through the curtained windows.

I check my watch. Rehearsal is in an hour and a half. There is the sound of a shower running and fresh clothes are spread across the bed. Slacks, a collarless shirt, and a casual but natty jacket I've never seen before. I turn on the television and switch to the History Channel. The army air campaigns of World War II buzz and snarl before my eyes while I wage my own tactical battle as to what my father was doing taking a sabbatical. What, I mean, besides watching television, reading poetry, and writing Nancy Drew mysteries.

I careen from one question to another, from one tentative answer to another. Is his hairlessness a result of a major depressive episode or of an alcoholic psychosis? It could, of course, be a response to stress or self-induced through shaving and the use of depilatory creams. As for the rash, it could be that he has developed an allergy to soap. That is the cause favored by Lydia and Dan. Egged on, I'm sure, by Mother, the patron saint of the double rinse.

In a burst of investigatory zeal, I skip down to the kitchen to count crushed beer cans and empty wine bottles in the recycling bin. Approximately half a case of beer plus three bottles of Chardonnay. Not that much. About what I am going through these first weeks of reconciliation with my lover. I wander to the alley and ease the lid from the garbage can. One sack of slops rests mournfully at the bottom. Spilled about it is a festive array of Chinese take-out cartons and withered condoms. Of course they cannot be condoms but plastic wrap from whatever he is eating these days. Twinkies, perhaps, or frozen Popsicles.

When I return to the bedroom, Father is dressed and tying his shoes. He has styled his cowlicks, trimmed his ears, and shaved his cheeks and neck. His eyes are bright and his face, at least, is clear of any rash. The line of his jaw is sharp as an axe and he is wickedly handsome. I smell aftershave lotion. I do not recall my father ever smelling— good or bad—before my mother left.

"Where are you going?" I ask.

"Out." His voice is dry with a hint of humor. "Isn't that what you've been pestering me to do?"

"But where?"

"I'm the father," he says. "I ask the questions."

"Okay." I feel my way slowly. "So. Do you have any questions?"

"No." He shoves his arms into the sleeves of his jacket and is halfway down the stairs. I imagine him leaping off the Aurora Bridge into the choppy water of Lake Union. Or he drives the Saturn (his choice of vehicle—Mother shepherds an ancient Jaguar) into a tree or simply (can suicide ever be simple?) steps in front of a bus. l close my eyes and the cartoon image of my father flies from the top of the 1962 World's Fair Space Needle and bounces from the roof of the lower level restaurant before slamming onto the concrete below.

I am being morbid. Cheerfulness and fragrant showers at the end of a depression often signal the victim has made the decision to quit living. Thus spake the reference books I've been reading in the library. They are conveniently stacked across the aisle from the tomes on autoimmune disorders. I am researching rashes. I will have to expand my search to include hairlessness.

"Wait!" I yell. "Are you going to see a doctor?"

His voice wobbles up the stairwell in an orgy of palsied echoes. "Turn out the lights when you leave!"

I am alone in the house I grew up in. I walk from bedroom to bedroom switching on ceiling lights and table lamps until the upstairs glows with false warmth. My mother was never much of a housekeeper, but in the months since she's been gone the cobwebs and dust bunnies have increased exponentially. Everywhere there is the musty smell of damp books and dusty carpeting. I do not recognize this house. It is not the home of my childhood.

In a snit of rebellion, I leave the upstairs blazing and move downwards to the main floor. Mail is stacked on the dining room table, several piles that slide into each other. The letter from my mother is on yesterday's pile and has been opened. It lies, face up, next to bank statements and second warnings on water bills. Mother's looping scrawl is as familiar to me as my own. The letter begins: *My God, Lee, have mercy....* and you can understand how it would be impossible for me to not read further.

> My God, Lee, have mercy and get e-mail like the rest of the world. Allene is driving me crazy. Will you please tell her what's going on? Tell everyone. Shit, take out an ad in the TIMES. I'm not happy with your decision but I've known it was coming for ten years. I, of course, have to leave the area—how can I stay here now?

She nattered on about last year's taxes and keeping the health insurance. The letter included a terse request that Father file for divorce since the whole miserable situation was his fault and she wanted to get on with her life without having to pay a lawyer and court costs. She ended by pleading with him to tell us, the children, about Rick. Or Rich. The ink was smeared with what might have been dried tears. Or spilled wine. Mother was not above a glass or three of Chablis before bedtime.

I squint at the page and read the letter twice, focusing on the spaces between the words. I stagger to the alley and drag the garbage can up the back porch steps and onto the back porch. I dump it in the middle of the porch. There, under blazing lights, I can see clearly that the plastic wrappers really are condoms. They nestle among the soggy tea bags, bright plum sauce, and crusts of toast. They glisten with the sheen of petroleum jelly and juicy sex.

Mother is right. He should have told us.

I look at my watch. I will skip second rehearsal. I do not know what—if anything—is wrong with my father, but I need facts about the dermatology of HIV, the progression of AIDS, and the requirements of cross dressing. I need such knowledge with the same intensity that I need oxygen. I lock the house, leaving every light on, and walk quickly to my car, to my own tangle of lies and desire. I am furious with my father's inability to speak clearly. He is a writer, for crissake. Can't he form a simple sentence?

I jerk the steering wheel to the right and pull my car to the side of the street. I am weak with fear for my mother's health. I do not want to be an orphan with no parents to love and rage against. I want my life completed by Mother's passion and Father's restraint. How can I balance myself without those opposing forces? Did my father endanger my mother? No. He wouldn't have done that. I know that with the same certainty that I know the sun rises in the east. I cannot bear to linger on the specifics and duration of my parents' sex life. Let Lydia demand specifics. I can't. Why, I ask myself, didn't Father tell us?

Pulling into the library parking lot, I realize that my father did tell. In his own way. I have a rash, he said. This is who I am. I neglected to listen to the silence between the words.

I will call him tomorrow. I want to meet your lover, I will say. I want you to meet mine. Her name is Beth and she's wonderful. I do not care if you have a rash. I will never abandon you. Don't abandon me.

Or perhaps I will simply ask if I should phone, now, before stopping by the house that used to be my home. I am the oldest, and I want to fix whatever is wrong with my parents but I can't. I never could.

Light Skin

Chimamanda Ngozi Adichie
21:2 (2003)

I knew what day it was by the smell from our kitchen. The food menu taped to our kitchen wall was on flimsy white paper—coconut rice and chicken on Mondays, beans and beef on Tuesdays, yams and greens on Wednesdays, jollof rice and plantains on Thursdays, *moi-moi* on Fridays. My mother changed the menu twice a year, wrote it on the same kind of paper, stuck it on the same spot. She liked order.

The houseboy did all the cooking except for weekends when my mother cooked, although she had the houseboy get things ready, like peeling onions and grinding peppers. When he made a mistake, like leaving too much skin on the beans for *moi-moi*, my mother shouted insults at him. "You brainless dark-skinned *muturu* goat"—"dark-skinned" sounding like the bigger insult. Or "Look at him, with skin as dark as the underside of a burnt pot," as though it was his dark skin that had made him do something stupid.

The houseboy always took it well, expressionless, and I felt that he believed my mother, that he was stupid because he was dark-skinned and there was nothing he could do about it. It was as though his expression, in its nothingness, said, Well, I'm dark-skinned; so what did you expect?

I, on the other hand, did not take being dark-skinned well. When my mother said, "You have my features, but how did you darken so much? Where did all that dark come from?" I fantasized about leaving banana peels on the stairs, so she would slip and break her light-skinned neck. She would say that every Sunday, while she stretched my hair for church. She placed the metal comb, with dangerous-looking big teeth, on the blue flame of the gas cooker for a few minutes, then she coated it with Vaseline that promptly melted and dripped off the comb anyway, before running it through sections of my hair. Sometimes she burned the tips of my ears or the back of my neck. I was not supposed to cry because those were small prices to pay for straight hair.

Years later, I would tell my students at Penn about the experience, and an African American student would tell me that they called it pressing and that many women still did it, the women who ran for cover in the rain so the straight hair would not revert, not tighten into its original kink.

On Mondays, when my hair bunched back up, sealing the bonds my mother's stretching had temporarily broken, my mother would weave my hair in corn rows and mutter about the thickness of my hair breaking her nails. Or say something like beauty is a tough thing to find if you're not born with it. She usually said it in Igbo, which was worse because the Igbo word, *esika*, actually lies somewhere between tough and impossible, does not have a perfect English equivalent. She would also say often, matter-of-fact, *ocha bu mma.* Fair skin is beauty.

My mother taught a course called Social Order to third-year students at the University of Nigeria. "We are the only people keeping this country sane, we academics," she would say sometimes as we watched television, in the same tone as *ocha bu mma.* "We are Nigeria's last resource; the military has squandered the oil and the iron and cocoa." My father would nod and mutter, "Yes, yes." He muttered yes yes to everything. He taught pure mathematics to postgraduate students and talked to himself in his study, so loudly that I heard him from downstairs.

Even before I was old enough to care, I wondered how they had met, how they had been attracted to each other. Now I know that my father was the only unmarried Nigerian man at the university in California where they had both gotten graduate scholarships from the United States Agency for International Development. Even then

Nigerians in diaspora believed they had to stick together.

They came back to Nigeria together—my mother with a straight hair wig and an American accent that she put on around people she considered important. They lined the hallways of their duplex campus house with bookshelves and they drank tea in the afternoons, even during the searing Harmattan, when the winds coated everything with yellow dust. They spoke a lot more English than Igbo to each other. They had a houseboy, a gardener, a driver, and a hairdresser who came in twice a month. They were members of the senior staff club and the tennis club. Nigerian academics. Nigeria's last resource. The ones keeping the country sane.

I must have come as a disappointment: a girl, and so sooty-skinned you could not make out my features from afar. Or at least that was my mother said. She wanted to have one child; she was too enlightened to fill the house with children, like people in the villages did. It was too Third World, that kind of behavior.

Perhaps to make up for my not being a light-skinned boy, she had me enrolled in the Children's Library, Girl Guides, the Block Rosary Crusade, the University Music Club, the right things of a child of Nigerian academics. I hated the blue Girl Guides hat, the way it always perched awkwardly on my head. And the military-style march we at the Government field on October 1 made me feel ridiculous, like an imposter soldier, made the muscles around my armpits ache.

Block Rosary Crusade meetings were on Wednesdays at the sacristy, thick with incense. I took short breaths as we said the rosary, scared I would deplete my share of air if I breathed too deep. At Music Club, the piano keys were unyielding under my fingers that never grew long and patrician, although my mother always tugged and pulled at them after she cut my nails. Plus I could not hold a tune. The other girls floated through, but the instructor stopped at me and tapped her ruler on the table as though to clear my voice.

The library was different. The crisp smell of new books that some foundation in America or England had donated, bearing the solid lettering of the foundation's name and their commitment to partnering with the University of Nigeria. The musty smell of the old books, the kind people's children donated, with pages browned by water and oil stains, sometimes with edges gnawed by mice or cockroaches or whatever. The metallic smell of the ceiling-high shelves. The calm smell of peace, of open doors to other worlds.

It was at the library that Chinelo and I became friends. I wanted to be her friend because of her skin. And her hair. Her skin—so fair her wrists turned red when she took off her plastic watch; her hair—soft, straight like brown sewing thread. Her ponytails fell elegantly, sloping; they did not tighten into kinky, stiff tufts like mine. Her father had not only come home with a London School of Economics degree, he had come home with a wife from Liverpool with eyes the wishy-washy blue of a hot afternoon sky. Chinelo was lucky; it was the Liverpool in her that softened the Nigerian hair, that blessed her with that skin.

I started to stand close to her in line, to hover near the shelves she looked at even though I no longer read Enid Blyton or Famous Five, until she noticed me. She would tell me later, teasing, that it was pity at first sight, at my sad eyes behind pink-tinted glasses. We started to go to the library together. "Race me to that tree!" she would say when we got out of the library.

She won every race. She laughed when she won and her hair bounced up and down, curly silk. I wanted to lose each race so that she would laugh, so that I could watch her hair bounce. Sometimes, I would rub my arm against hers as we walked. Of course, I knew it was silly, even then. But I did it anyway.

She lived on Ikejiani Avenue, a street away from me, and her mother walked around the house in a T-shirt and nothing else and raised rabbits in the living room upstairs, red-blonde hair falling across her face. She spoke halting Igbo and taught religion and laughed loudly and cried when Chinelo's father killed a spider. Once a mouse nested in Chinelo's pillow—she had settled into bed when she felt her pillow quiver—and her mother built a cage so Chinelo could keep the baby mice. I wished she were my mother.

The library was close to the junior staff quarters where the secretaries and drivers and cleaners lived in row homes so cramped that next door became quite literal—you could stand outside your front door and stretch out and touch the handle of your neighbor's door. There were no shapely lawns hugged by rows of flat-trimmed bougainvillea, no spacious yards hemmed in by tended frangipani trees.

When we raced, Chinelo and I stopped at the mango tree right before the first row of homes. The mango tree was diseased, with mottled leaves and fruits that never ripened before rotting. They went straight from an unyielding green to a dead brown, never turned yellow or reddish-purple. We always stopped at that tree; going farther into junior staff quarters meant going into unsafe territory. Kidnappers lurked there, my mother had told me years before when I first joined the library, towering men who wore socks over their heads, holes hacked in them for eyes, and who had raffia bags slung over their shoulders to collect the heads of children.

I no longer believed my mother when I finally went past the tree. I was in grade six, already sporting breasts the size of palm kernels, and had read Soyinka's Jero's Metamorphosis. Still, fear shot through me when Chinelo first suggested we go in. "I don't think we should," I said. My mother didn't even know that we raced to the front of the row homes.

"Come on, let's just see." Chinelo was already leading the way, her spongy hair floating behind her. The same way it had floated, like bunches of gold thread let loose, when she climbed the slender avocado tree in our backyard that was out of bounds for climbing because it did not have any supportive lower branches. She had hugged the trunk tight like a lover and slithered up, snake-like, until she got to the branches.

"Come on, Ona!" Chinelo said.

I followed her. The walls of the houses had mud-brown patches, from children kicking soccer balls against them, like a polka dot design. Papers, broken furniture, Coke bottles, old crates were stacked against the walls, clear of the common yard behind. Some boys were playing soccer at one end of the yard. They had dug short sticks into the ground to create goal posts. On the other end, a bunch of girls played *oga*. Years later, I would literally hop around in class and demonstrate *oga* to my bemused American students and tell them that it might be considered a variant of hopscotch.

But I was not concerned with the *oga* players that day. I was staring at the boys playing soccer, at one particular boy playing soccer. He was staring at me too. I knew he wanted to come over and talk to me, but then the other boys noticed Chinelo and me and ignored their flabby soccer ball to stare at us.

"*Nee anya*, what do you want here?" A goalkeeper shouted, in Igbo. "Where is your driver?"

"*Ajebo!*" Another screamed.

I still do not know exactly what *ajebo* means because it is borrowed, not an indigenous Igbo word. But it connotes pretentiousness and privilege—people who speak through their noses like the British and drink Earl Grey tea and go abroad on vacations.

"They are coming from the library, library people!"

"They speak only English! They don't hear your Igbo!"

"They eat only cake and milk. No *akpu* and *garri!*"

They taunted us for a while until he stopped them. I knew he would. In the romance story bubbling in my head, he went on to beat them all up, single-handedly, for taunting his beloved.

"Leave them alone." His voice was quiet; he was the kind of boy that all the other boys listened to. The boys shrugged and went back to their soccer. Uppity senior staff children were not enough to stop their game for too long.

"Let's go and play with the girls," Chinelo said.

Was she crazy? The girls would beat us up. Their eyes already sparked with angry flames when they saw us. We were senior staff children who went to the primary school on campus with polished wood chairs while they went to the primary school in town that had no windows, only gaping rectangular holes in the walls.

"Chinelo, we have to go home. My mother might wonder where I went," I said.

"She'll think you're at my house. I'll tell my mom to tell her you were."

I let Chinelo persuade me, I didn't want to leave anyway. I wanted to stay and stare at him.

"Can we play with you?" Chinelo asked.

She would die many years later during a pro-democracy protest in Lagos when the soldiers started shooting. She was in front of a group of demonstrators, and when a soldier came close to her, she said something to him, with a smile. A win-you-to-our-side smile. But the soldier shot her. It was the same smile she used with these girls. It worked, and we started to play with them. They played a rougher, brisker version of *oga*; it was possible to get viciously kicked during play. My handclapping and leg movements were not always in harmony; I stared across the clearing too often. He was staring too. I heard the boys grumble about the goal opportunities he missed.

He came over a moment later and signaled, and Chinelo started to walk toward him. He had signaled for Chinelo, he had been staring at Chinelo. I forced myself to look away, to focus on the tips of the trees with the rotting mangoes. The other girls kept playing as though nothing had happened. Even Chinelo acted nonchalant; she just walked over to him. Back in our neighborhood, a boy walking over to talk to a girl would have caused a sandstorm of giggles, pinching, jabbing. Few of the boys in my neighborhood would even talk to a girl like that. They were all wrapped up behind thick glasses and video games and baseball caps their parents had brought back from America.

Chinelo stood talking to him, leaning against a whistling pine tree. I tried to concentrate on the *oga*, tried not to stare at them. The word we used then was "rap." It was clear he was "rapping" her and if she agreed, they would leave together; if not, she would leave the tree alone.

They left the tree together. He walked us out of the yard, toward the mango tree with mottled leaves.

"My name is Odunze," he told me, in English. Close up, he seemed a year or two older than us. His face was so smooth the dusty scar under his nose was a relief, hooked, as though some metal had torn into his flesh. He was smiling, in the way a teenage boy smiles at the best friend of the teenage girl he likes.

"I'm Ona," I said.

Chinelo walked between us, slowly, stopping to pick off grassy spikes that had gotten stuck to her trousers.

"What books did you get from the library?" he asked Chinelo.

"I just returned some books. It's Ona that gets books all the time. You should see the big fat books she reads," Chinelo said proudly.

I wanted to cry. I wanted to run off and not stop until I got back to Cartwright Avenue, to our duplex surrounded by well-tended bougainvillea, to the familiar food smells from the kitchen. Anything other than to be the nerdy, dark-skinned friend with the glasses who reads fat books.

"I wanted to join the library but I can't because my father is not a senior staff. He is the vice chancellor's driver," Odunze said.

I nodded, as though to apologize.

"Have you read Anthills of the Savannah?" he asked, looking at me.

"Yes."

"Me too. But Things Fall Apart is still my best."

"Mine too."

"Let me see your book," he said, and when I gave it to him, he ran callused fingers over the wrapped book. All the library books were covered in cellophane. "Most of the books I read don't have covers, some don't even have the first and last pages," he said.

"Oh," I said.

"Race me!" Chinelo yelled then. I didn't race. I watched them race, watched her straight hair flying in the wind. He held back so she would win.

If I had not made the decision to be child-free, I would be close to my child; I would know when my twelve-year-old child was in love. I would talk to her, I would see the misery behind her glasses and hardcover books, and I would know that it was an unrequited love. Perhaps I would even guess that her light-skinned friend had won the boy. Now, I imagine what my mother would have said if she had known—the son of a common driver! Common in the same tone as dark-skinned. It would not help either Odunze *was* dark-skinned.

Perhaps my mother didn't suspect it was a boy because if it was a boy she thought she would know him—it would be somebody's son, somebody she and my father knew from the senior staff club. Somebody with a houseboy and gardener and driver. There were boys like that who liked me then, even with my dark skin. There was Obisike who lived on Fulton Avenue and walked like Chinelo's guinea pig when he fell off his new chopper bicycle. There were others. But during what my mother later chose to call my difficult adolescence, when I read and read and read, I wanted only my best friend's boyfriend. I didn't want to like anyone else.

I wrote tortured poetry and hid the pages under my mattress. The houseboy found them once, while he cleaned my room, but I did not panic, I simply took them and re-hid them. Years later, I would tell myself that I had internalized my mother's views: I thought that because he was dark-skinned, he was too dumb to know what the poetry was about.

Odunze and I were friends in the way that you are friends with your best friend's boyfriend. We talked about books. We laughed at Chinelo's jokes and intrigues, at how naïve she sometimes was, how giving. Perhaps it was why I could not hate her, for being light-skinned and being Odunze's girlfriend, everything I wanted to be. She would still be my best friend if she had not died.

Still, when her mother decided to move back to England because her father got a second-year student pregnant, I was happy. Chinelo was not. We were almost sixteen, and she had started to raise her voice to her mother, to say things like, "Go put on a bra, Mom" and "If you weren't so scattered, he wouldn't go chasing young girls," but she could not refuse to go with her mother. "I will be back, I will come back when I am old enough to decide for myself," she swore.

And she did, years later. But by then my family had left Nigeria. And she would die shortly afterward at the hands of the soldier. Even now, when I think of her, I can still smell their house—the smell of strawberry soap that her grandmother sent from England, the smell of wet rabbit fur, the smell of elephant grass.

I knew Odunze would not fall into my arms. I knew I would have to pursue him. I was sixteen, old enough to want to seduce, but too dark-skinned to seduce with my looks. So I used books.

The first few times, we sat outside, on the cracked steps of the row homes. His friends stopped by but soon slouched off, the girls to go gossip and listen to music in somebody's cramped room, the boys to watch porn tapes or read the lewd Lolly magazine. They said hi to me and talked to Odunze the rest of the time. I understood. It was impossible to transfer feelings for a light-skinned girl, a half-caste at that, to her charcoal-skinned friend.

Odunze teased me. *Sisi*, he would say, you go to Music Club to learn piano. See, your *ajebo* legs are not used to mosquito bites. You can't sit on the stairs without placing paper down first? Will your legs break if your driver does not drive you to school? But he had not teased Chinelo. Maybe it was because we were younger when they first started. Or maybe he thought Chinelo had every right to be an *ajebo*, a white mother and light skin justified her privilege. When we talked about Chinelo, it was always with a certain reserve, as though we knew we straddled a delicate line that we had to be careful not to cross, to either side.

One day, he asked me to come inside. The living room was so dark that the naked bulb dangling from the ceiling was turned on in the afternoon. There were way too many objects in the room to let any sunlight through—fans, pots, trays, cartons, tables, mats, kerosene lamps, plates. A house cramped into a room.

"What are these for?" I pointed at the stacks of the Guardian and Daily Times on a three-legged table that leaned against the wall. He told me his mother fried *akara* and sold the bean balls in the student hostels. She collected old newspapers to wrap the *akara*.

"I will get your mother some old newspapers. My father has stacks in his study," I said.

"No."

"Why?"

"Just no."

After that, I knew not to offer any favors, and even when I brought him books, I pretended that I needed somebody to discuss them with, that I had not merely brought them because he did not have access to the library.

He started to ask me in each time I came. We would sit in the shadowy living room, dust particles swimming fog-like around us, talking books. We communicated with our eyes, or I imagined that we did. Mine lingering on the pimples on his forehead, his dwelling on the cuticles of my fingernails, the ones my mother shoved in and I nibbled out.

One day, he said, "Chinelo and I didn't do anything. She didn't let me get past her breasts."

I could hear his mother at the back, pounding beans in a mortar. They did not have a kitchen—the kitchen was the kerosene stove outside that spewed thick gray fumes when the wick thinned. He led me by the hand into the only bedroom in the house. A bag of rice, some sickly yams, and a tin of palm oil leaned against the wall. The bed was narrow, the worn lines on the sheets looked like they would give with one more wash.

"What if your father walks in?" I asked.

"He won't be back soon. He drives the Vice Chancellor to work, then the Vice Chancellor's wife to the hair salon, then his children to the library. Do you know Ifeyinwa, his daughter?"

"Yes." I nodded, suddenly ashamed that I knew her, that I sometimes went over to her house.

He turned me around, pushed me against the wall. The smell of palm oil filled my nose as he whispered "relax" in my ear and fumbled down there. It occurred to me even then that it was not me he wanted, that it was Chinelo in my body, that he was not starting something but finishing it or, at best, continuing it. Yet I did nothing as he shrugged his trousers down to his ankles and pulled my dress up. He parted the slice of underwear between my legs. For a few moments, he seemed lost to everything, to the stuffy oily room, to his mother outside, to me, to Chinelo. And in the middle of my discomfort, I felt powerful.

The sex got better. We advanced to talking. We explored Achebe and Soyinka and Laye while his thrusts got faster and faster.

"Okonkwo was guilty of believing too much in the way things should be," he would whisper, in between moans.

"Ekwefi is the symbol of sacrifice," I would say. "Yes, sacrifice. Sacrifice! Sacrifice!"

After sex, after he cleaned up the wetness between my legs with tissue as stiff as writing paper, he would say, "I will get rich one day. I will use Star tissue."

"Will you marry me then?" I would ask.

"Why not?"

And I would look in his eyes and know it was a lie. Because he did not say "yes," he said "why not?"

There was a sense of things falling apart that year, the year I was seventeen—things getting worse, slipping away to a place you could never reach out to bring them back, to put them back up. There was the coup, and the new head of state promised reform, but then magazine editors started to disappear, the ones who wrote critical pieces. They stopped importing wheat, to encourage local production in the north, and a friend of my mother's, just back from a study leave at Berkeley, wrote a guest column about how the head of state's family ate bread imported from Britain. A week later, she was imprisoned. My mother complained at dinner every night that even the academics, the only ones keeping the country sane, were being bullied, and my father said, "Yes, yes."

I started to use bleaching creams. At first, I mixed Ultra-Glow and Shirley, and every morning I dashed to the mirror to check my face. They were too mild, Igna who owned the beauty shop in the market told me; they were for people already light-skinned who wanted to be lighter. So I started to mix two different bottles, one called Special Lightening Cream, the other Fairy Beauty. Both were in moldy-looking bottles, the words on the labels so blurred I could not read where they were made. Both promised light skin in a week.

I didn't know, I didn't know, was what my mother would

say years later, when I confronted her with the patches of purple under my eyes, like dry burns, the rest of excessive hydroquinone. *You knew,* I would shout back at her. Some of those creams even had mercury! Mercury!

But then, I did not know that my nightly rituals destroyed the melanin in my skin as well as my skin's top layers, that they put me at risk for skin cancer, that when I had the car accident, they would make it nearly impossible for the doctors to stitch the gash on my chin.

Odunze noticed that I was lightening up. He said, you look fine. And I smiled quietly and plotted to look even finer, even lighter. Things were changing in his house too; the bags of rice and beans that leaned against the walls slowly disappeared. The container of palm oil never looked refilled. His mother cooked with firewood now, she could not afford kerosene. Then the university lecturers went on a nationwide strike and his mother stopped selling *akara*. There was nobody to buy.

One day, at dinner, my mother said, in between mouthfuls of coconut rice, "We are leaving next month, we are going to America."

"Why?" I asked.

"Things will never get better. The standards and buildings of the university are crumbling fast, nobody's funding the university anymore, nobody cares," my mother said.

"Yes, yes," my father said.

"You think they care that we are on strike? Their children are in universities in America and England. Why should they care? Look what is happening," my mother pointed, as though if I looked toward our sideboard I would see what was happening in Nigeria. "Students are buying degrees, and even the prices of those are falling. Our friends have all left, the staff club is so empty these days."

Silence hung over the hallways of our house, cast a pallor over the heavy bookshelves as we packed. My mother wrote letters of recommendation for the houseboy and gardener and driver and gave them some of our old clothes. Now I wish I had paid more attention to them, especially the houseboy. He was with us almost ten years, yet I cannot remember what he looked like, what shape his face was, if he ever smiled.

I cried on the way to the airport, throughout the flight to New York, and for a long while after that, I cried because I did not want to leave home, and I cried because Odunze had not even come close to crying when I told him we were leaving. He said all *ajebo* families would leave eventually anyway. I wrote him laboriously, every other day—detailed, sensory letters from the apartment in Ann Arbor, Michigan, that my parents rented for six years until they bought a house.

Years later, when I had my short memoir published, some of my students read it and asked why Odunze couldn't just leave Nigeria, join me in America. And I said, "Because he didn't have that choice." Not that he would have wanted to, at least not because of me.

Then though, because I did not fully realize this, I asked Odunze in my letters to try to leave, to go to the American Embassy, to apply for a visa. He addressed it only once, with a stiff question. "Do you think Americans give visas to poor people?" His letters finally stopped coming, like a slow tap that drips and trickles until the water just dries up.

I saw Odnuze recently—now, twenty-six years later—at Ifeoma's wedding. Ifeoma grew up at the University of Nigeria too, although we were not friends then. Like many of my friends here, we are friends because we have Nigeria in common, because Nigerians in diaspora become friends when they detect the familiar accent in a grocery store, marry each other off to other Nigerians, fly across America just to attend a fellow Nigerian's wedding or child's christening. Her husband is Nigerian too, introduced to her by another Nigerian at another wedding. Nigerians in diaspora sticking together.

Floor-sweeping caftans in blue and green, flowing *bou bous*, orange and red wrappers and blouses dotted the north Philadelphia wedding hall. After the American-style catered dinner, the guests settled down for the main fare, the jollof rice and *moi-moi* and fufu. I had decided to pass on the jollof rice—I did not know how many points to award it on my new Weight Watchers plan—when Odunze walked up to me.

"Ona?" he asked. He had grown a huge beard, warlord-like.

"Odunze. I can't believe it's you."

We hugged like old friends, touching bodies, thumping backs. He was loud, perhaps a little tipsy. He narrowed his eyes looking at me, and I knew he disapproved of my dreadlocks, and the cowries strung through them, of the dark patches of skin that I had not bothered to hide with foundation. Battered skin recovering from hydroquinone and mercury.

"How are you, Ona? Long time."

"You stopped writing."

"Long time," he said again, as though he had not heard me.

"You stopped writing."

"I had problems. My family, going to school, even eating was hard. Life was hard."

"It was hard for me too."

"*Ajebo* like you? You always had it too easy."

I shrugged away the jibe, examined his face. His skin was still too smooth, even with the beard. A mustache covered where the scar had been, and I felt a perverse pleasure knowing that if I reached out and pried the brown hair aside, I would see the scar. "How long have you been here?" I asked.

"Fifteen years. I live in Delaware. I am an accountant. I do some consulting on the side."

"I thought you would be an English major."

"English majors cannot put food on the table." He

smiled and I thought how smiles did not change in twenty-six years. "How about you?"

"I was an English major. English doctorate too. I teach African literature at Penn."

"You could afford to study English."

"I took out loans for school. My family never had that much."

"Much is a relative term," he paused. "How is Chinelo? Are you still in touch?"

"She died. Seven years now."

He looked away, silent for a long time. Then he shook his head. "I did not know. I moved up north, to Kano, soon after you left. I never heard from her."

I shouldn't be, after so many years, but I was happy that I knew this one major thing about her that he did not.

"We were in touch. She was happy, I mean before she died," I said.

He shook his head again; his eyes dimmed as he stared across the wedding hall. I knew he could not see the couples swaying to Nico Mbarga's "Sweet Mother," the woman who was hastily retying her loose wrapper, the toddler who was wailing, looking around the dance floor in bewilderment.

"I know what you mean. Like my father," he said finally. "He died last August, but he was happy. I sent them to London two years ago on holiday. Guess who was on their flight, seated close to them? The Vice Chancellor."

If he wasn't married, I would think about visiting him, letting him push me against the wall of a spacious room in his suburban Wilmington house, letting him wipe between my legs with tissue afterward. Charmin, or some other soft brand. But I would not do it.

His wife is white, Irish American with blue eyes and hair the color of corn tassels. They kept clutching each other, sipping from each other's wineglasses, both smeared with the ripe tomato color of her lipstick. And his children were there, two boys with the exact same shade of skin as Chinelo.

You Know the Killing Fields

Willa Schneberg
Storytelling in Cambodia (2006)

—for Rada Long, interpreter

She believes because I am Jewish
I must understand
what she went through after Cambodia
was ground down to zero on April 17, 1975,
when grim-faced teenage boys
wearing fatigues over black pajamas,
grenades, pistols, rifles, rockets
weighing down their shoulders,
marched cocky into Phnom Penh.

I must understand how the Angka found her
in the paddies in the moonlight stuffing rice kernels
into her pockets to keep from starving
and bashed in the back of her head with a shovel.

I must understand that they frisked her,
found the eyeglasses inside her *krama*
and smashed them into the monsoon-soaked soil,
raving:
*Traitor, intellectual relic, you can't run from
the "Super Great Leap Forward"* and then slashed
her arms with the shards of broken glass.

I must understand why they threatened
to cut out her tongue for humming
a snatch of song sung by Sin Samouth,
the Frank Sinatra of Kampuchea,
who is nothing more to them
than a bourgeois capitalist pig

masquerading as a Frog.

I do not tell her I wasn't there,
that I read about the Holocaust like any goy
who wishes to understand.
Instead, I tell her about a Nazi who sat at a table
covered with delicacies and booze,
holding an automatic pistol in his hand,
who forced Jews to lie naked face down in a pit
and between shots of cognac shot them dead . . .
as if it were my story.
She says, *You don't know how happy*
you make me, you know the killing fields.

Note: Sin Samouth was lured back to Cambodia from Paris to be a leader in the "revolution" and was then murdered.

Freer Than I've Ever Been

Teresa R. Funke

This story is an excerpt from Funke's book Dancing in Combat Boots: Stories of Ameri-can Women in World War II *(Bailiwick Press, 2007).*

I only whistled cuz I was bored. Me and Josie leanin' out the window of the barracks, two young colored men walking by. We were on the second floor and I didn't think they'd hear me, but one looked up, and Josie and I bolted back to our bunks, holding our sides. Hester said, "You girls are too fresh for your own good," and we laughed some more.

"Come on, Lucy. I'm hungry," Josie said, so we told Hester we were headin' over to the mess hall, if that was okay with her. But when we jumped out that door, there they were—tall, handsome boys in their army uniforms. "Well, the WACs are lookin' good today," the skinny one said.

"Was that you whistled at us?" the other one asked. He was a sergeant with broad shoulders and big arms, but he had an easy smile and I liked him. Josie started to answer, but I gave her a nudge. A woman's gotta keep her secrets.

"Where you girls headed?" the skinny one asked.

"Mess hall."

"Well, we'll come along then."

I put my hand against the sergeant's chest. "You know you can't eat with us 'cept on Sundays. The mess sergeant has to count you in."

He took my hand and held it for a moment, with just enough pressure to show he meant business and not enough to make me think I oughta worry. His hands were calloused, like the sharecroppers' sons back in Richmond County.

"Come on, girl. We're hungry. Why don't you go in

there and get us a sandwich?"

I stood there looking hard at him. My father once told me you could read a man's thoughts in his eyes. It was the only such thing he ever told me, so I've held it close and taught myself to look. This young man had a smile in his dark brown eyes and nothing else. Josie took my sleeve and pulled me into the mess hall, but I looked back over my shoulder at that big man, and heard his friend call him George.

"Hey, Nettie," I heard Josie say, "fix us up some sandwiches. There's a couple good-lookin' Joes outside say they hungry."

Nettie stole a look from the window and put her hands on her hips. "Y'all go and get yourselves caught up with men you know nothin' about. You're gonna get your brains beat out one of these days if you're not careful."

I put my arm around her and drew her toward the counter. "That's why we're takin' 'em some grub, Nettie. To get a feel for 'em. Now don't that seem wise?"

Nettie just grunted. She made up the sandwiches though, and I noticed she didn't skimp on the mayonnaise like she sometimes does with us. Now wouldn't that make Mama mad; Nettie here layin' the mayonnaise on thick, and Mama back home doin' without, just like I'da been if I hadn't joined up. Now *I'm* the one the country's scrimpin' to feed, and if they thought about it at all, wouldn't that make those white ladies back home think twice about all those fats they been savin'?

We sweet-talked Nettie into makin' us a sandwich to share, cuz you should never eat big in front of a man you're tryin' to impress, and we stepped out onto the lawn, and that's how those two boys, George and Marlin, come to ask us to the movies tonight.

From the time I was a little girl, I saw how hard my mother struggled just to keep us kids in shoes and I said, this isn't my kind of life. I didn't know how I was gonna get away from it, though. I really didn't. All the boys had gone off to fight Hitler or the Japs, so wasn't no husbands to be had. I wanted to go to normal school in Fayetteville to become a teacher. I'd always admired my teachers. They'd come up the hard way, like the rest of us, but could sure make do in that cold, cramped classroom of ours with those used-up books handed down from the white kids. They were the reason I could add sums in my head faster than anyone in my family, the reason I kept my nose in a book and out of trouble. Thought maybe I could make enough money to put one of my little sisters through later, but Daddy said no. He didn't have no money to be sending no girl off to school.

My brother was callin' for me to come up North. Lots of our folks had gone, but for some reason that didn't sound right to me either. At the time, I was workin' for an old lady who paid me five dollars a week to cook, clean, and do her laundry. One day she sent me off to the post office and I saw these two recruiters—pretty white girls in beautiful uniforms—and I was struck. And when I stopped to talk to them, they smiled at me like I was their equal. I listened to what they had to say and rushed back home to tell Mama and Grandma. They was bitterly against me joinin' up, though. Said all them women were in the service for prostitution, but I didn't believe it. Next thing Mama and Grandma knew, I had signed up and was off to Des Moines, Iowa, for basic training. I look around now and know they was so far from right about these girls. The whole country's wrong about us, but we're showin' 'em.

"Hey, Hester, loan me five dollars," I say.

"Lucy, whyn't you ever got money of your own?"

"Cuz she spends it fast as she gets it." Josie has a laugh like the trill of a songbird, and it makes me giddy just to hear it.

I sit down on Hester's bed and lay my hand on her knee. She's our master sergeant but acts like a mother hen. "Now, Hester, ain't it al¬ways you tellin' me never to go out broke? I'm just followin' your good advice."

Hester throws my hand off and pulls her face into a pout, but she reaches into her blouse and takes out a five-dollar bill. "Keep this in your bra, and if those fellas start actin' funny, you girls call a cab and get yourselves home."

I stand and smooth my skirt over my back side. I'm wearing my good uniform, my tropical worsted jacket and skirt, chamois gloves, garrison cap, and my civilian pumps. Uncle Sam even thought to outfit us with a nice brown handbag. "How do I look?"

"You fill it out good," Josie says.

I look to the others for approval. There's Olive from Maryland. She's a licensed beautician with smooth, light skin, and I never go out without her checking my hair. And Luella from D.C. She said she worked at the Pentagon for a time before she quit to join the service, but she won't say why, and we all wonder. There are the girls from Mississippi that came straight off the cotton farms like me, and Margaret, an uppity gal from Atlanta that comes from a family of doctors. There's Chloe, who ran away from her husband, and them two girls in the corner sittin' too close to each other. I look past them, and past Sally too. She was a college instructor up North before the war. I think on account of her education someone promised her something to get her to join up and whatever it was never materialized. She's disappointed and bitter, and I steer clear of her. And then my eyes land back on Josie, who's here for the same reason as me, to shake loose the tight reins of her mother. They may not be high society, and I may not like 'em all, but they're good women. They take the flack that Uncle Sam throws at 'em and hold their heads high. They aren't afraid of hard work cuz that's all they've ever known. For the first time in my life, my world is bigger than Richmond County, and Mama may not say it, but I believe she's proud.

I know it's not ladylike, but I can't stop myself lookin' at George. I look at him through my glass when I lift my beer and out of the corner of my eye when I'm supposed to be listenin' to one of Marlin's stories. I look at him square on when he talks to me cuz I want to see that smile in his eyes and the casual way he moves his lips, like he's got nothin' but time. I like to watch him when he laughs. He's not one of those men who throw their heads back and let it all fly; he's more the type to drop his chin toward his chest and shake his head while a chuckle shakes his shoulders. There's nothin' showy about this man, and I like that. I really do.

I can hear Hester telling me that I'm too young, and I don't know men. She thinks because I lied about my age to get into this army that I'm still a child she can boss, but I'm twenty-one, and I've dated enough fellas in my two years in the service to know a thing or two, and that don't make me loose, just lucky. There's not a soul alive wants to spend all their time drillin', sloppin' chow in the mess hall, takin' orders. It's not expected for the men to hold back when they're off duty, so why should we girls behave any different? But that don't mean I just fell off the turnip truck; I know enough to push away the new beer Marlin just ordered for me, for example, but I'm not ready to wind down yet, not by a long shot.

The others are doin' what soldiers always do—white, black, male, female, don't matter—they're gripin' 'bout the service. I'm more than happy to join in.

"The women who recruited me made it sound like the Army was going to be a rosy, rosy thing," I say. "Them in their fancy uniforms. Not like the mismatched, drab, ill-fittin' pieces they gave us colored girls when we joined up."

"You said it," Josie says.

"You know, them recruiters didn't mention how we'd be fallin' out at four o'clock in the morning, drillin' 'til breakfast, scrubbin' the floor, makin' up the bed."

"When that colonel come by and run his white glove cross the top of your locker, girl, it better be white when it come down," Josie says.

I thump the table. "Flip a quarter on your bed and it better bounce."

"Clothes better be hangin' every piece just so." We laugh. "No, sir. Not what I expected."

"Well, then, why'd you join up?" George asks, and he's watching me so close my chest hurts cuz I can't get a breath deep enough to fill it.

"Well, there wasn't nothin' for me in Richmond County 'cept being a maid, maybe workin' in a laundry. That's all they'd let us do. All our men were off to war, and I was related to half of 'em anyway." He drops his chin and chuckles, and I reach for my beer again just to give my shaking hands something to do.

"Yeah, so now you can work in *Uncle Sam's* mess halls or his bakeries, maybe clean *his* hospitals," Josie says.

"Don't forget the motor pool," George adds, and we all laugh. We'd all joined up thinkin' things would be different, but things never really are for us, and we shoulda known that. Like right now we're sittin' round the corner from the first diner we tried out tonight, the one where the owner pushed past his pretty blonde waitress to stop us at the door and tell us we weren't welcome. Even after all these months, we still slip into thinkin' that things might be different here Up North or Out West or whatever you want to call Fort Lewis, Washington. We thought our uniforms would make a difference, that us all being in the same war together would matter somehow. Damned if we didn't get ourselves fooled again.

"No, sir. Not what I expected," I mumble into my glass. "But it got me outta North Carolina. And when the war's over, I'm gonna use the GI Bill. Get myself an education."

George raises an eyebrow, and for a second I think he's gonna be like the other men, gonna say something stupid 'bout how a woman should be home raisin' babies. I've got myself so convinced that I raise a finger to his face to stop him talkin', but he takes my hand and lowers it gently to the table and just holds it there, and now I know I'm feeling something I didn't feel with the other GIs.

My mama used to say if a man looks at you when you're talkin', you got his full attention, but she didn't tell me that don't happen often. Most of the guys I been out with sit with their chairs pushed back, one leg stuck out into the room, their sides to me. I know they hear me talkin' cuz they grunt or nod, sometimes laugh, but their eyes are not on me. They're searchin' out buddies from the base, watchin' for white soldiers who've given 'em trouble, keepin' an eye out for officers. Their eyes are busy starin' down old white farmers and young white business¬men, checking out the teenage girls at the counter and wait-resses in their starched pink uniforms. But not this man. This man's sittin' with his legs under the table, his feet flat on the floor, his hand holdin' mine, and his eyes on me; and I'm realizin' when this fella ships out, I just might cry a bit more than usual.

Before Fort Lewis, I was stationed at Fort Huachuca, Arizona. There were a couple of black divisions there— the 93rd and then the 92nd Infantry Divisions—and those men were gettin' trained to head over to the Pacific and later to Europe. Troop trains pulled out of Fort Hua¬chuca loaded with some of America's best young, strong, black men. A few of them had my name and address in their pocket. Many of them never came home.

There was a four-foot wall on the base made of concrete, and we used to sit up on that wall and talk to the young men. Our company commander told us not to, that it wasn't ladylike, that we should bring them on into the day room instead, but we'd still hang out there on that wall. That's my best memory of Fort Huachuca. Us girls sitting out there on those warm Arizona nights, the moon shining pretty and bright, and it was like a party out there, laughin' and talkin' with the boys who were going off to war. I'm average height, and I've got good skin and a nice waistline, but I've never had anything special to make me stand out. When I was sittin' on that wall though, I *felt* like I was somethin' special. We all did, and there was no harm in that. We'd waited all our lives to feel that way. And then one night the company commander took her flashlight, and she walked that wall and said no¬body better run. She lined us up and confined us to barracks and that stopped us hanging out on the wall, but that's how I'll always think of Fort Huachuca. That's how I'll always remember those boys I wrote to who didn't come home.

And I'm thinkin' 'bout them today cuz the caliber of colored men here in Fort Lewis isn't nearly so high. Most of these fellas are with engineering groups. They're trained to build bridges and roads, and they're a bit rougher round the edges, and I've been more careful since I come to Fort Lewis, but that George is different. He asked me to accompany him to church yesterday mornin', and that kinda surprised me. I guess it speaks well for what kind of man he is, and Hester says I deserve a gentleman. But he's no stick-in-the-mud either. After church, he came back to the barracks, and we shot pool in the day room, and every time I came up to shoot, he made me laugh so hard I scratched the ball. After he ate with me last night, he asked could he call on me again. I know he's shippin' out soon, and I oughta say no. A girl falls in love with a soldier who's shippin' out and she's bound to either get her heart broke or wind up married too young, and I don't want either. I got plans for my life. I almost told him no, but I didn't, or I should say I couldn't. I couldn't say no, and here I'd come to think this army life had made me stronger.

Truth is I haven't felt this unsteady since I first stood on that parade ground at basic training, listenin' to some white officer lay down the law, and wantin' badly to go home. Now I'm not sure where home is anymore. Richmond County seems so far away, and the girl I was seems like an old friend I've lost touch with. But someday this war is gonna end and Uncle Sam is gonna send me home to North Carolina, back to Mama and Grandma and all those other folk who think they know what's best for me, and I'm wondering if maybe, just maybe, it'd be nice to have someone around who'd love me for who I am now, somebody like George.

So my mind is spinning now, and it's hot out here on the parade ground. They say it doesn't get hot on the Puget Sound, but it sure is today, and I'm hungry and tired from marchin' and I wanna sit down, but we're waitin' for the two white battalions to enter the mess hall first, and I hear myself say, "If we're in the same army, why do we have to wait? Aren't we just as hungry as them?" But I didn't realize how loud I said it till our sergeant turned and stared me down and said, "Because it's tradition for whites to enter first, that's why." And that was the end of the discussion.

That's where it always ends and it don't ever get easier to swallow, but it made me realize something—what we want and what we get are two different things in this life. If George ships out and never comes back; if the war ends and I marry that man, settle down to a house full of kids; if I take that GI Bill and make myself a teacher, it'll happen like it's gonna happen and me sittin' here worrying won't change a thing. He's a hard-workin' man, he treats me with respect, and knowin' he's somewhere on this base right now makes me feel a bit lighter, like a Sunday hymn. So when our battalion finally starts to move, I raise my eyes up over the camp lookin' east toward home, and I let all that anger and worry go because they don't belong to me any more than the future does. And I don't wanna feel them anyhow, because the truth is whatever happens when this war ends, here and now, far from Richmond County, I'm freer than I've ever been.

Ratification

Allison Green

27:2 (2012)

1972

1. Hawaii

My third-grade teacher, Mrs. Peerenboom, tall, gangly, and wrinkled, said of course we didn't want the Equal Rights Amendment to pass. If the ERA passed, girls would have to go into the jungle and handle snakes. She looked at pug-nosed Denise. "Do you want to have to go into the jungle and handle snakes?"

2. New Hampshire

We were talking about the ERA because it was the front page story in the Weekly Reader, a children's newspaper that came to our class. That week the first states had started voting on whether to ratify the amendment. The ERA, depending on your point of view, would either make sure women were treated equally to men or send the world spiraling to a fiery hell in a very small basket. The wording was clear, once I understood what "abridged" meant: "Equality of rights under the law shall not be denied or abridged by the United States or by any state on account of sex."

Denise's pug nose quivered like a rabbit's.

Mrs. Peerenboom looked down at her: "That's what you'll have to do if the ERA passes. Go into the jungle and handle snakes."

3. Delaware

I went home and asked my mother what she thought about the ERA. Mom had dropped out of graduate school when she got pregnant with me, but Dad continued his studies. Now he had started his first tenure-track job here in Green Bay, and Mom was staying home with my brother and me.

Mom said the ERA was a good idea. It meant women were as good as men. I didn't understand why, if it was that simple, people like Mrs. Peerenboom didn't support it. When Mrs. Peerenboom brought it up, I said nothing. But I was sure it would be ratified. I was sure the people who thought women were as good as men would win.

4. Iowa

The ERA didn't spring up out of nothing in the 1970s. It was first introduced to Congress in 1923. Women's right to vote had just been secured through the 19th Amendment, and Alice Paul, a suffragist, thought the Constitution ought to protect women's rights in general. She wrote the first draft.

5. Idaho

The Senate finally passed the amendment in 1950. The House did not follow. The Senate passed it again in 1953. The House of Representatives finally passed it in 1970. The House passed it again in 1971, and the Senate followed in 1972.

6. Kansas

Now it was up to the states to ratify it. Ratification required the approval of thirty-eight states within seven years. If getting Congress to pass the amendment was a boxing match, then ratification by the states was mud wrestling.

7. Nebraska

The meaning of women's equality was debated on all my favorite television shows. On "The Brady Bunch," Marcia insisted that girls were the same as boys and talked her way into the boys-only Frontier Scouts. She passed all the tests on the camping trip—barely—but then decided she'd rather read fashion magazines than build a fire. On "The Courtship of Eddie's Father," a young feminist took the handsome widower on a date. She insisted on opening doors, tasting the wine first, and paying the check. When she wanted to stop the role reversal and pursue their romance, she got her comeuppance. Tom kissed her and then lectured: "Equal. Equal but not the same. Equal but different. And as far as being a man is concerned, I'd give up the act if I were you. It really isn't a very good one . . . There's something in the basic man-woman relationship—"

"Oh, yeah," she sighed, eyelashes fluttering.

"—that's worth keeping. Remember that."

8. Texas

I didn't try to join the Boy Scouts or open doors for boys, but I did worry about how to act in class. It wasn't good for a girl to be too brainy or too talkative or too loud. Even though I frequently knew the answers, I made sure not to raise my hand too often.

9. Tennessee

Articles about the ERA continued to appear in the Weekly Reader. Some people said that if the ERA passed, prisons and dormitories could no longer be segregated by sex. Priests would have to bed with nuns and sorority girls with fraternity boys.

10. Alaska

The ERA would require women to be drafted, people said. This at a time when many men didn't want to be drafted either.

11. Rhode Island

And what if judges couldn't assume, when deciding custody, that mothers made better parents? Indeed.

12. New Jersey
Jail sentences: Men and women wouldn't get different sentences under the same circumstances.

13. Colorado
And then there was the issue that really made people squirm. The ERA, some said, would mean men's and women's bathrooms would be "separate but unequal" and therefore unconstitutional. Mrs. Peerenboom asked if we girls wanted to share bathrooms with boys. Denise sent a sidelong glance at stinky Roger and gagged, but I didn't believe Mrs. Peerenboom.

14. West Virginia
Jury duty. Men and women would have to be treated the same.

15. Wisconsin
Admission to public schools: Women wouldn't be held to higher standards than men, and vice versa. As if vice versa had ever happened.

16. New York
Mrs. Peerenboom was retiring that year. In the spring, she gave away things from her desk to the winners of the spelling bees. The day I won, she gave me a pencil holder that was made of a frozen orange juice can wrapped in felt. I threw it away.

17. Michigan
The summer of 1972 was long and hot. My parents rented a house on a more pleasant street, and I went down the block to find someone to play with. A group of kids ran around someone's front lawn, playing and wrestling. A boy about my age had two tennis balls and a beach ball under his shirt. He pranced, holding up his pregnant belly. I said, "That is offensive to the female sex." The other kids

looked at me and went back to wrestling. The boy acted like he hadn't heard.

18. Maryland

Fourth grade began, and Mrs. Neitzel divided the bulletin board at the back of the room. On one side she posted anything we brought in for Nixon and on the other side she posted anything we brought in for McGovern. The Weekly Reader asked us, "Should a woman be president of the United States?" My peers voted, overwhelmingly, "No." About that time I took to wearing Oshkosh overalls and clod-hopping boots. I stood on the edge of the playground, my arms tucked in the bib of my overalls. Something was going on, shamefully, on my chest.

19. Massachusetts

Some said the ERA was not compatible with the teachings of the Bible. They said women were born to serve. To serve men.

20. Kentucky

Some said the ERA would open the door to gay marriage. I didn't know that fifteen years later, I would want such a right.

21. Pennsylvania

Some argued that the 14th amendment, which says citizens should be treated equally under the law, was enough to protect women from discrimination. The Supreme Court had ruled in 1971 that Idaho couldn't give preference to men in handling estates, and it based its ruling on the 14th amendment. In the decision on Reed vs. Reed, we find that a boy died in 1967 sometime after his parents separated. Both parents applied to administer his estate (the mother, should she prevail, would be called the "administratrix"). According to Idaho law, "of several persons claiming and equally entitled to administer, males must be preferred to females, and relatives of the whole to those of the half blood." Mothers, that is, were the equivalent of half-blood relatives.

22. California

At the open house, Mrs. Neitzel showed my parents the bulletin board. The Democratic side, she said, was a testament to my determination: I contributed every poster, flyer, and doorknob hanger on that side of the board. My parents wore the rueful grins of perpetual losers. Even Richard Nixon supported the Equal Rights Amendment, but it would not be enough.

1973

23. Wyoming

Republican activist Phyllis Schlafly woke up one morning and thought:

No one is doing a darn thing to stop this Equal Rights Amendment. Guess it falls to a woman to do it. As usual.

24. South Dakota

Phyllis Schlafly of the shellacked hair and red suits and pearls. She got on every radio station, every television station, every college campus. She was willing to debate anyone, anytime. She preached ERA apocalypse.

25. Oregon

I got used to seeing Phyllis Schlafly on TV. She reminded me of Mrs. Peerenboom, but with suits instead of sweaters. She had that same tight mouth. Sometimes her opponents wore pantsuits and ties that made them look like men, and sometimes they wore turtlenecks and jumpers that made them look like harried kindergarten teachers. I rooted for them. But Phyllis Schlafly looked so sure.

26. Minnesota

Joanne, who lived on the other side of our duplex, became my best friend. Her parents were divorced, which was uncommon, and my parents sometimes talked about how hard it was for Winnie to raise three kids by herself.

27. New Mexico

One day Joanne and I were playing a board game in her room, when her mother burst into the house, followed by her friend Linda. We peeked into the living room. Winnie was furious. I had never seen such fury. In a skirt and blazer, she paced back and forth, swearing. She seemed not to notice Joanne and me, crouching in the doorway. Linda sat on the floor, nodding, murmuring, not trying to calm her down, just showing her she was listening. It took me awhile to understand that Winnie had gone to a job interview for a bank manager position. When she got there, the man said, "We have the perfect job a girl like you." Secretary. She'd gone all the way up to Menominee for that. To be treated like that.

Joanne and I slunk back into her room. I threw the dice.

28. Vermont

Often, on the black-and-white nightly news, Walter Cronkite or John Chancellor or Harry Reasoner would give an update on ratification. States that had not ratified the ERA were a darker shade of grey. The South was a clot of resistance.

29. Connecticut

On the same day that Connecticut voted to ratify, Nebraska voted to rescind its earlier ratification. In all, five states would rescind their approval. This kicked off a long legal battle over whether rescission was possible.

30. Washington

It no longer seemed inevitable that the ERA would be ratified. Phyllis Schlafly smiled her righteous smile.

1974

31. Maine
The Florida House would vote for the ERA one, two, three, four times, but the Florida Senate would vote against it seven.

32. Montana
Fifteen states never ratified it. Thirty-five states did. Three short.

33. Ohio
When I was a baby, women couldn't get a loan, buy a house, or start a business without a man's signature. Before I could legally drink in a bar, the word "post-feminism" had been coined. The era between pre-feminism and post- was no wider than the kerning between two letters on this page.

1975

34. North Dakota
Some say the ERA fight, though the amendment failed to pass, had a positive effect. Marcia Brady got people talking, shifted the culture. A generation of women was mobilized into political action. Congress passed laws in response to specific injustices; in 1974 it became illegal to discriminate against women in housing and credit.

I survived the loss of the Equal Rights Amendment by listening to the "Free to Be You and Me" album; dreaming that I was Harriet the Spy, the girl in my favorite book; and hiding in my overalls. But an ulcer of doubt burned in my stomach—not doubt that I was as worthy as any boy, but doubt that the world thought so. If I wanted to make it, I had to keep my thoughts to myself and be wary of betrayal.

In the first pages of my first diary, in 1976, I recorded an evening spent with two boys my age at my grandparents' house. We watched a cartoon based on a Rudyard Kipling story, about a mongoose that saves a family from a cobra snake. From the conversation afterward, one would have thought those boys wanted to go into the jungle to handle snakes. I kept quiet. And that night I wrote, "It's always the same thing. The boys do the talking and you go along with it and nod and laugh. I wish I wouldn't do that! But every time I'm with a boy I try to please them. I'm never myself."

1977
35. Indiana
The ratification deadline was in 1982, but the ERA had died long before. Suffragist Alice Paul died with it, July 9, 1977. Phyllis Schlafly is still alive.

THE UNLEVEL TABLE

Women's Work

Anthropologists call it kinship work. Feminists defined the term "second shift". History has called it women's work and has failed to see the beauty and power inherent in the traditionally female work of family, food, caretaking, and illness. Admittedly tedious, backbreaking, and often heartbreaking, CALYX authors have explored the work of family and community as an essential part of the human experience. And we don't just mean the selfless and sainted—women's take on their labor can be bitter, resentful, or just plain gruesome. Its power comes from its realness, its tedium, its repetition, and its heartbreak.

Western literature ignores the work of child-raising, of cleaning and feeding a family, of caring for relationships and community, preferring for these tasks to be sanitized or carried out offstage—nonessential to the plot or character. Or, when stories focus on the labor of women they are relegated to "chick-lit" and given candy-pink covers that scream "don't take this seriously, this isn't real literature." But these are the stories of our lives, of our humanity, and of our future. Critics love a good "discovering what really matters as death approaches" story, but not the realities of death—the mess, the incredible physical labor of caring for the dying, the conflicting emotions, and the clinical indignity.

These collected pieces aren't necessarily about family mechanics, but they are pieces that, at their heart, are embedded in family, responsibility, and the work of community. Through births, tenderness, growing pains, illnesses, long slow descents, and deaths, we trace the arc of cultures and civilizations, of humans and humanity. Caring and kinship work—this so-called women's work—isn't ancillary to the creation of culture: it is at its very core.

The Middle Daughter

Barbara Kingsolver

If you threw her in the water
she would float upstream.
What if baby Moses had floated upstream,
bobbing up toward Lake Victoria
in his little bullrush boat,
passing the transfixed laundry women,
leaving them behind in a wake of amazement?
What then would have become
of the Children of Israel?
This middle daughter forgets, there is always history.

If you show her white, she says
she only sees black.
There has always been this problem
with her vision.
From infancy, she has thrown off
every color we wrapped her in:
first the pink, contemptuous,
and later even the blue, for reasons
we hadn't the nerve to be thankful for.
She says she wants to wear red, or nothing.
And you should see her with her red shirt
flapping on her little spindle body
like some solo flag,
marching up the river,
leading the salmon to slaughter.
She says they aren't really dying.

She says that something is born of swimming
upstream
that finds its way back to the sea
and spreads like a grassfire through the seaweed
across the floor of underwater continents

and finally comes back to the very same river,
not one, but a thousand fish,
a generation of fish.
This middle daughter believes
she will make history.

MEMORIES FLOW IN OUR VEINS

My Mother Combs My Hair

Chitra Banerjee Divakaruni
Black Candle: Poems About Women
from India, Pakistan, and Bangladesh (1991)

The room is full
of the scent of crushed hibiscus,
my mother's breath.
Our positions are of childhood,
I kneeling on the floor,
she crosslegged
on the chair behind.
She works the comb
through the permed strands
rough as dry seaweed.
I can read regret in her fingers
untangling snarls,
rubbing red *jabakusum* oil
into brittle ends.

When she was my age,
her hair reached her knees,
fell in a thick black rush
beyond the edges
of old photographs. In one,
my father has daringly
covered her hand with his
and made her smile.
At their marriage, she told me,
because of her hair
he did not ask for a dowry.

This afternoon I wait
for the comments,
how you've ruined your hair,

this plait's like a lizard's tail,
or, if you don't take better care
of it, you'll never get married.
But the braiding is done,
each strand
in its neat place, shining,
the comb put away.

I turn to her, to the grey
snaking in at the temples,
the cracks growing
at the edges of her eyes
since father left.
We hold the silence
tight between us
like a live wire,
like a strip of gold
torn from a wedding brocade.

The Decedent Is Initially Viewed Unclothed

Marianne Villanueva
19:2 (2000)

The body was that of a "well-developed, mildly obese Filipina female." "Moderate muscular rigidity" was observed. The temperature, it was noted, was "cool." The lividity was "posterior and purple."

The scalp was "atraumatic." The "brown irises had equal 5 mm pupils." The lips were "free of abrasions." The "natural dentition," it was noted, was "in good repair." The ears were unremarkable.

The chest was "symmetrical." The breasts were "free of masses." There was an inch-long area of "purpura over the dorsal area of the right foot." There was "pronounced cyanosis of the toes." The hands were "atraumatic."

"Stepwise dissection" of the neck revealed "focal hemorrhage into the fascial planes."

The gastric contents consisted of "approximately 60 ml of greenish black fluid. "The pylorus was noted to be unremarkable. The small and large bowels were "without note." The rectum was "atraumatic."

The heart weighed 350 grams. It had a "smooth epicardial surface." The right lung weighed 1,330 grams; the left, 1,100. Over both lungs were areas of "purulent exudate." "Confluent abscesses filled with yellow-brown material" were seen in both lungs. *(Somewhere I read that, between them, the lungs contain about 300 million tiny air sacs whose combined surface area equals that of a tennis court. When you breathe in deeply, the bases of the lungs extend to the depth of the tenth pair of ribs in your body.)*

The liver was approximately 2,030 grams. The hepatic vein was "yellow-brown and speckled a rich nutmeg color."

(Was the doctor a poet? What words he used—) The pancreas was firm; the gallbladder was free of stones.

The right kidney weighed 300 grams; the left, 350. The kidneys had "finely granular subcapsular surfaces." A cross section of the renal cortices, medullae and pelvic calyceal systems *(Did they slice her open, from end to end?)* showed no focal lesions. The ureters were of normal caliber. Examination of the internal genitalia was unremarkable. Her endometrium was described as "thick and hemorrhagic." Her vagina was unremarkable.

Her spleen weighed 200 grams. A cross section of the splenic artery showed it to be "severely congested and mildly autolytic."

I asked a friend, a heart surgeon in Minneapolis, to explain to me the meaning of words like epicardial, extravasated, subarachnoid, basilar. She said, "Send me the report of Case No. M91-9915." I waited then. Her news came back: "Basically," she told me, "your sister died of heart failure."

My mother went to the morgue. Later, she told me about it. There was a toe tag on my sister's right foot. Her hands were bound. She was wrapped in a winding sheet. When I called from California, the day after her death, I asked my mother, "Could you get a piece of her hair for me? To keep?"

My sister was going to be cremated. My mother said, "I want it done quickly." If I hadn't asked my mother this, there would have been nothing, nothing of my sister's to hold on to.

In the morgue, my mother cut locks of my sister's

beautiful long black hair. But not before stroking my sister's hands and noting the mauve nail polish, applied only two weeks before.

"You know," my mother told me later, her voice rising with amazement, "she looked so beautiful. She had gone back to her old size, not that swollen shape she'd been in the hospital, when they were pumping her full of hydrocortisone. I recognized her again."

My mother gave a few strands of hair to me; the rest she kept for herself.

I tried to read the autopsy report six months later. It was the end of a hot day. The hills were dry and brown. Voices carried from the outside. I was alone on my deck, in the Santa Cruz Mountains, in the beginning of a dry summer. Hawks circled the pale blue sky. I heard their shrill and mournful cries. The cat hunted in the tall grass below me. Sometimes it would bring me trophies: rabbits, rats, once a gopher. My son was at camp. My husband hadn't returned from the office. Then, the line that stopped me from reading was the first: *The decedent is initially viewed unclothed.*

I put the report away.

Years later, in September, I found it again, buried underneath a box of old papers. I started to read and found it beautiful, this exploration of my dead sister's body, its description of the wrinkled mucosa of her esophagus, the color of her gastric mucosa identified as "light beige," the yellow-brown of her hepatic artery—all this so much more eloquent than the body they pulled out of a drawer in the morgue to show my mother, when she arrived from taking my sister's children to school. I finger the report's nine pages, examine dates, pore over the doctors' signatures.

And in the end, my friend was wrong. It wasn't heart

failure: why did she lie? There it is, the words clear as day at the end of the report: "sepsis as a result of necrotizing pneumonia."

At the end of the typed descriptions, a handwritten report of a microscopic examination of the brain, written by a Dr. Angelina P. Szper. Angelina! *(An angel dissected my sister's body.)*

And there, finally, is the peace I'm looking for: in the frontal lobe, "an acute hemorrhage about a necrotic vein," "fibrinous thrombi in nearby vessels." The splenium: "multiple small hemorrhages and infarcts." The cerebellum: "scattered acute hemorrhages and necrotic vessels." I want to know this because it tells me that perhaps, perhaps it was better that my sister died.

Portions of the brain are saved in a stock jar.

(If I go to the office of Dr. Szper in Manhattan, will she still have portions of my sister's brain in a jar? Will she show it to me?)

In the house in Manila where my sister and I lived as children, our bathroom was a long narrow room with an uneven tiled floor. The one window faced out onto a vacant lot. Sometimes we saw a little boy hunting among the cogon grass of the lot. Once he brought us a black snake and said he would sell it to us for five pesos. I paid for the snake from my allowance and stuck the bottle with the snake in the freezer. I forgot about it for a couple of days and the snake slowly froze. One day the cook screamed. She had found the bottle, and the snake's eyes had turned glassy and gray.

When my sister and I brought a puppy home from the animal store, and the puppy died, drowned in the goldfish pond, my sister put the carcass in a bottle. Floating in formaldehyde, its little paws pressed close to its body, its white hair undulating slightly in the yellowish liquid, the puppy, whose name was Percy, seemed almost alive. It looked at us with a beseeching expression. My sister took it to her biology teacher and received an A that semester. After that, the other girls in her class vied with each other to bring in things in bottles. One girl brought something her uncle, a doctor, had given her. A strangely deformed fetus, with what looked like two heads growing out of a stalk-like neck. The biology teacher, Mr. Mapua, placed the bottle on a windowsill and the light coming through the window made the fetus' skin almost translucent.

I had a squarish body, a thick neck, and a round head that was flat as a board below the crown. Everyone remarked on the flatness of the back of my head, though because my hair was so thick one would have had to actually press on my head to notice such a thing. But it seemed that, in my family, everyone knew this about me. Everyone talked about it all the time: my sister, my grandmother.

When my grandfather was very old, the back of his head, too, began to assume that misshapen flatness. It reminded me of very young babies, when their heads are soft and malleable. When I rested my hand on the back of his head, it was soft and rather lumpy to the touch. That was when I began to think there might be something wrong with him. And only a few weeks later, he was dead, dead of a stroke.

I always thought I'd be the first in my family to go.

Six days before Christmas, my sister checked into the emergency room of Lenox Hill Hospital on Park Avenue, complaining that she had trouble breathing. The nurses made her sit down and gave her a glass of water. At the end of eleven days, while I was at work, a call came from my aunt. "Your sister—" she said . . .

I couldn't support my head anymore and had to put my forehead down on my desk. After a moment or two, a high-pitched wail erupted from my throat, a sound even I didn't recognize. My little office quickly filled with people. "Baby, oh baby," said Myrna Chiu, holding my head against her chest. "Oh baby, you've been hurt. What is it, what is it?"

Years later, I saw her in a supermarket. The Safeway right near my house. It was late afternoon. The store was crowded. There were maybe five people in each checkout line. I picked the line where the last person looked like they had the least number of items, but of course it was the wrong line. No one moved for maybe twenty minutes.

And then I saw her. She was directly in front of me. Her long black hair, curly and wiry, giving off glints of light. The dark eyebrow, like a wing over the white, white skin. She was with a much taller man, who had to bend down to hear what she was saying. As she talked, her hands moved in the air.

What I saw of her was only the hair, the right eyebrow, and the gestures. My heart leaped. Before I could stop to think, I found myself murmuring, "Oh, I have *missed* you."

I looked and looked, taking in every detail of the animated being in front of me. Then she was finished with her groceries and was hurrying out of the store, hurrying because the man with her was taking such long strides and would soon pass her. I wanted to run after them. I wanted to say, *"You—"*

Cabeza

Monique De Varennes
20:1 (2001)

None of them, not even Barbara herself, quite understood why she brought the pig's head home from the market. She had browsed in the meat department's hooves-and-hearts section many times—Variety Meats, it was euphemistically called—but she had never before been tempted to buy. For one thing, she had no idea how to cook the innards and extremities whose red or pink or tannish flesh jammed the display case. For another, she had always felt that looking was quite enough.

And she did look, nearly every time she visited the market. She loved the colors and textures of the meat: the deep red coils of spleen, the lacy tripe, the kidneys like weighty, dark bunches of grapes. She liked to see the thick slabs of tongue, so surprisingly large and muscular that she wondered how they fit in an animal's mouth, and the pigs' feet, small and achingly dainty, like a society matron's helpless, manicured hand.

The pig's head, though, was altogether different. It was the first one Barbara had ever seen in Variety Meats, and it had her attention from the moment she laid eyes on it. It had belonged to a young pig, a piglet, she surmised, for it was not very big. Whitish, sightless, it wore an expression of great seriousness, as if it fully recognized the gravity of its situation. It seemed isolated there in the case, separated by shrink-wrap from the neat neighboring packages of organs and hocks, some of which were undoubtedly its own. It looked lonely even, and impulsively Barbara popped it into her shopping cart.

Driving home, she smiled with pleasure at the thought of her purchase. No exile in the dark recesses of the meat keeper for this baby; she would make a place for it at the very center of things.

But even when she had settled the head front and center on the refrigerator's middle shelf, pushing jars and leftovers aside with rare abandon, she felt that something was missing. The pig looked as mournful of countenance and as forlorn as ever.

Barbara got busy. She brought out a white serving plate, and, stripping off the head's wrappings, set it carefully in the center. Some lettuce leaves gave color to the dish, and she accented the green with a sprinkling of cherry tomatoes. Briefly she considered stuffing an apple into the pig's mouth, but she discarded the idea: it would give the head far too rakish an air. Still, she could not resist draping one sprig of parsley over the pig's right ear.

She set the plate in the refrigerator and stepped back a few paces to contemplate the effect. The pig looked less gloomy now—almost cheerful, in fact. And if its gaiety seemed somewhat forced, well, at least she knew she had tried her best. Satisfied with the disposition of the head, she closed the refrigerator door and forgot about it entirely.

Two hours later, hearing the kitchen door slap shut behind her fourteen-year-old, Barbara remembered. No greeting, of course. No call of inquiry, drifting down to the basement where Barbara folded laundry; Carol had abandoned such pleasantries a good two years earlier. She now communicated rarely, except to express displeasure. Upstairs, kitchen cabinets slammed as she hunted for an after-school snack.

Barbara dropped the T-shirt she was smoothing out and rushed to the foot of the basement stairs. "Carol, honey, before you open the refrigerator, there's something I—"

But she was too late. Carol's shriek ripped through the air, a blade of sound. Barbara dashed upstairs. She found Carol standing squarely in front of the refrigerator, her eyes fixed on the closed metal door. Barbara put awkward arms around her daughter.

"What is that? Mom, what's in there?" Carol demanded, shaking free of her mother.

"It's a pig's head—a piglet's, really. I bought it at Ralphs."

The words sounded strange to Barbara. Clearly they sounded strange to Carol as well, for she gave her mother one brief, dark look and fled abruptly from the room. A moment later, Barbara heard a door slam in the far reaches of the house. She opened the refrigerator.

There sat the head, all innocence, clearly incapable of hurting even a fly. Really, she couldn't see why Carol was raising such a fuss. In any case, she had no time to contemplate the question now. There were piles of laundry still to fold, then there was dinner to be made. She thought pork chops would be nice, though she realized the choice showed a certain lack of sensitivity. She would serve them on a lovely bed of saffron rice.

It was not Barbara's habit to make the same mistake twice, and as five thirty neared she kept alert for the sound of the garage door. Jed she did not have to worry about, at least not yet; he had soccer practice nearly every afternoon during the season and rarely made it home much before dinner. But she did not want Peter to be surprised. Her husband did not do well with surprises. She settled down distractedly for a look at the newspaper.

It was nearly six when she heard the sound of Peter's car. Barbara folded the paper neatly, taking care to smooth out the creases she had made, then wandered as casually as she could into the kitchen. Carol must have been listening for Peter too, for when Barbara entered, her daughter was already there, and Peter, briefcase in hand, was bending close to hear her whispered voice.

"A what?" he exclaimed. He did not seem to notice that Barbara had come into the room.

"A pig's head, Daddy—I swear. She got it at Ralphs. Check it out for yourself."

Peter opened the refrigerator impatiently, as if

anticipating some particularly stupid prank. Then a small sound escaped him, something between a grunt and a groan, and his back slowly stiffened. He stood absolutely still. After eighteen years of marriage Barbara knew that silence, that utter stillness; he was busy rearranging the unpleasant into some form that suited him better.

After a moment he seemed to shake himself, and he reached in for the pitcher of whiskey sours that Barbara always had waiting for him when he came home from work. "Well, Carol," he said finally, "I don't see that this is anything to get excited about." His voice was bland. "Your mother is probably planning to make cabeza."

Carol's pointed, freckled face sharpened a bit in disappointment. Clearly she had hoped for a scene. "Cabeza?" she repeated sullenly. "What's that?"

"A traditional Spanish dish—a kind of stew, I believe."

"She's planning to cook it? To make us eat it?"

"I never said I was going to cook it. Never uttered a word about that," put in Barbara, who had begun chopping up a crisp napa cabbage. The pork was baking nicely. But they did not seem to hear her.

"Well, she can cook it any way she wants," Carol continued. "I'm not touching it."

"Touching what?" Jed banged in the kitchen door and swung his backpack to the floor.

"Look in the refrigerator for a preview of tomorrow's dinner. Mom's going Spanish on us."

Jed followed Carol's suggestion, gazing for a moment into the antiseptic brightness of the refrigerator. Then he reached behind the head for a bottle of Gatorade. "Weird," he murmured appreciatively. "When Mom's done, can I have the skull for my room?"

Not much more was said about the pig's head that evening; Peter effectively glowered them all into silence. But it was he who brought up the subject as Barbara was getting ready for bed. She knew what he planned to discuss from the moment he cleared his throat. Stretched out on the mattress, his reading glasses perched atop his head like a second set of ears, he had the same look of strained forbearance he'd worn the day he had dissuaded her from filing for divorce, three years earlier. His voice, when he spoke, was low and calm. "About the cow's head, honey—"

"Pig's head," Barbara corrected promptly. "It's a pig."

"About the pig's head. Are you planning to cook it or not? Because if you're planning to cook it, I personally will eat it and encourage the kids to do the same. But if you're not, I think you ought to consider—" and here he appeared to be sorting rather carefully through his words "—disposing of the thing."

Barbara received this suggestion in noncommittal silence, though her bones froze at the thought of throwing away her pig. She watched Peter's face grow increasingly intense, and she knew he was struggling with something. "Why did you buy it?" he blurted out at last.

Barbara considered this for the first time, rather surprised that it had not occurred to her to wonder until now. She did not dare tell him that the pig had looked lonely, and that was not, she guessed, the whole truth in any case. "I don't know," she said finally.

For a moment she thought, I should try to talk to him about it. Who else, after all? The children were still too young, and no one outside the family could possibly understand. She looked at him, exposed on the bed, his rough, hairy legs poking out from smooth pajama bottoms, his stomach wearing the soft bulge of middle age. He looked vulnerable, approachable. Then his face hardened, and that was all she could see.

"Never mind why you bought it," he said gruffly. "I don't even know why I asked. Just deal with it, Barbara, won't you?" He flicked his glasses down from his forehead to cover his eyes again, as if closing himself to any further conversation. And that was that.

Next morning, Barbara noticed that the upstairs bathrooms needed cleaning, and she spent a couple of hours working on them. She was the sort of housekeeper who always let things get a little disreputable before she cleaned, so she could experience the small satisfaction of seeing her scrubbing and polishing make a difference.

Later, over a sandwich, Barbara paged through her cookbooks, looking for a recipe for cabeza. She was not quite sure that such a thing existed. She knew that the word meant head in Spanish. She also knew that Peter was quite capable of inventing a dish if it helped smooth over an awkward moment in his day. Certainly none of her foreign cookbooks—of which she had several, left over from the days when she had truly enjoyed her time in the kitchen—made reference to it. The Larousse Gastronomique came closest, with one recipe for brains, one for the snout, and no fewer than eight ways of fixing the ears.

The very thought of cutting into the pig's head aroused anxiety, and Barbara brought the platter out onto the kitchen table and sat down in front of it. Today it looked scoured and sere and somehow wise. Peter was right to ask: Why had she bought it?

She stared at it hard, trying to understand. Its presence seemed to overflow the kitchen. It was, for her, utterly there, more than her cookbooks or the salt shaker or the Pothos on the windowsill, whose small green life she had nursed for nearly fifteen years. She was aware that the head aroused in her a tangle of feelings, and that those feelings were quite strong. But when she tried to separate them so that she could name them—name even one—they eluded her, vanishing in wisps of emotional fog.

She looked at her watch—an entire hour gone. There would barely be time to throw some caramel custard together before Carol got home from school. Barbara thought she would make a double batch; caramel custard was Carol's favorite.

By the time she heard her daughter's step on the

driveway, Barbara was a bit apprehensive. But to her surprise Carol did not seem inclined to be hostile. "Did you cook the head yet?" she asked bluntly.

Barbara shook her head.

"Well, that's a relief." Carol sniffed the air avidly; she still had a child's unerring radar for sugar. "Hey, something smells sweet."

"Caramel custard. It's for dessert tonight, but there's extra, if you'd like a snack. In the refrigerator."

Barbara watched Carol's mouth tighten as she contemplated the refrigerator uneasily. She smiled a bit as her daughter pulled open the door and quickly withdrew a dish of custard. This Carol bore off, wordlessly, to her room.

That night neither Peter nor Jed mentioned the pig's head, though both of them asked, almost upon entering and with enormous wariness, what was for dinner.

"Chicken," Barbara answered primly, and each refrained from commenting on what she had not cooked.

The next morning, as soon as the last of her family had left the house, Barbara took out the head again. A faint odor had begun to emanate from it and its garnish was past its prime. Barbara removed the wilted greens (the tomatoes were still serviceable) and sprinkled a little Arm & Hammer on the plate before tenderly laying a new bed of fresh lettuce. She patted the top of its skull. "You might smell a little off, but you look just fine," she reassured the piglet, smiling at it warmly. Then she wrapped it in heavy layers of Saran Wrap and returned it to its shelf in the fridge.

She did not take it out again, but the knowledge that it was there eased her through the day. She greeted Carol that afternoon with a plate of freshly baked cookies.

"You're cooking a lot these days," her daughter commented as she filled a glass with tap water.

"For some reason I've just been in a kitchen mood."

Barbara registered the water in her daughter's hand. "Don't you want some milk?" she asked solicitously. "I was thinking as I baked these cookies how tasty they'd be with a tall, foamy glass of milk."

"No, this'll be okay." Carol's eyes jerked nervously toward the refrigerator, and Barbara could see that she had no intention of opening that door. So, helpfully, she threw it open herself, revealing the gleaming shelves, the milk carton, the pig's head. "Come on, have a glass."

When Carol had retired—rather abruptly, Barbara thought—to her room, it occurred to her that no one had been visiting the refrigerator much, not since the head had come home. Last night, Jed hadn't made his usual late-night food raid. And Peter hadn't even gone for his nightly whiskey sour; she had found the pitcher untouched on its shelf this morning.

Her observation about the refrigerator was confirmed that evening at dinner, when it became clear that she had not set out horseradish for the pot roast. This combination was traditional in their family; Peter had been known to become quite irritable if they were out of the condiment on pot roast night. But tonight no one mentioned the missing horseradish. It was always, of course, possible that they did not notice, but somehow Barbara doubted it. She sat in quiet amazement, watching her uncomplaining family eat their pot roast unadorned.

The evening passed without incident. Only Peter mentioned the head, commenting in an offhand way that she might want to make that cabeza soon if she was planning to cook it at all; he didn't think that kind of meat had much of a shelf life. Barbara responded with an alert and agreeable nod.

She had noted with interest that the family was tiptoeing around her, humoring her. Peter was his usual reserved self, yet there was a guarded solicitude in his treatment of her that she had never noticed before. Jed, the charmer of the group, had begun to favor her with doses of his incredible smile. Even Carol had been almost polite. Barbara wandered through this atmosphere in a mild fog, curious as to what would happen next.

Three days passed. No one spoke to her about the head. One morning she got up early and, as always these days, went straight to the kitchen. Even before she opened the refrigerator, she could smell it. The odor was stronger now, and it was not pleasant. She pulled out the platter and, holding her breath just a bit, patted a thick layer of Arm & Hammer on every surface of the head. It gave the thing a ghostly look but seemed to tamp down the odor considerably.

Barbara had long ago abandoned the garnishes that surrounded it. The lettuce lay flat and black on the plate, the tomatoes were dimpled with softening dark spots, and the once jaunty parsley was little more than a smear along the piglet's cheek. Ignoring this, she doubled the sheath of Saran Wrap, masking the smell.

By the time Jed came in she had coffee going. A bowl of pancake batter was at the ready by the side of the stove. She could tell from a tightening around his eyes that he smelled the pig too, but still he offered her his rich smile." So, Mom, you want to come to my soccer game this morning? Dad and Carol are coming, and we're thinking of going out to lunch after."

"Oh, I couldn't possibly. I'm making a terrine of veal for dinner and it takes forever. If I don't start early we won't eat till midnight. Besides, isn't this a school day?"

"No, Mom," Jed said gently, "it's Saturday. Come on— you haven't been to a game for ages. It'll do you good to sit out in the sun. We can have burgers for dinner, for all I care."

But Barbara demurred. She had too much to do here, she insisted; the dinner ingredients were bought already. Besides, she had seen him play a hundred games and would see a hundred more—she could miss just one. Finally, Jed was forced to relent.

Barbara enjoyed her day. When the kitchen had been cleared of breakfast things, she set a pot of spices simmering on the stove to freshen the air. With the cheerful bubbling in the background she made her stuffing, chopped and marinated her meat, lined her terrine with pork fat, and artfully filled it with layers of the stuffing and veal and ham. It was the first time in ages that she had taken real pleasure in cooking. She glazed oranges for dessert while the terrine baked, and while it cooled, made arranged salads and cold rice. It would be the perfect light supper for her family.

They all, however, displayed a striking lack of appetite for dinner. They talked loudly—with more animation than usual, Barbara thought—but they only picked sporadically at their food. Perhaps they had eaten too much, or too late, at lunchtime. It was fortunate that she'd decided on a cold dinner, one that would keep—for days, if necessary—in the refrigerator.

That night, Barbara went to bed early. But the sound of crying pierced her dreams, and with a mother's instinct she got up, stumbling across the darkened bedroom, to offer comfort. The light was on in Carol's room. Even from Barbara's doorway down the hall she could hear her daughter's voice, raised in weepy complaint. Was she babbling to someone on the phone at this hour? A small twist of annoyance infiltrated Barbara's concern.

As she approached the door, Carol's words came clearer. "It's just so weird. She spends all of this time cooking—cakes, cookies, fancy dinners. And there's that head, just rotting in the refrigerator. It scares me, Daddy." She sobbed loudly, her breath ratcheting.

Barbara felt excitement trickle through her, and was invigorated. Crouching in the dark hall just outside the doorway, she settled in to listen.

"I know it seems odd," Peter replied, his voice steeled to

calmness, "but you have to look at this from your mother's perspective. She bought the head to cook it, naturally, and for some reason she just hasn't. Maybe she's embarrassed about that. And—"

"And what, Dad?" Jed broke in. So it was a full family conference. "And she just leaves it to rot? Face it, Dad, there's something wrong with this picture. Mom's gone over the edge."

There was silence for a moment; then Jed spoke again, his voice strained and determined. "I don't know about the two of you, but I'm not eating another thing that's been sitting in there with that head. And first thing tomorrow I'm going to talk to Mom. I'm going to find out what she's been thinking. This is crazy, going on like this, pretending nothing is wrong."

Carol began to cry again. This time, Barbara could hear real pain in her sobs. She knew that Carol's face would be red and slick with unwiped tears, that her shoulders would be heaving, that her hands, forgotten, would lie limp at her sides. It was the way she had always cried as a child. As far as Barbara knew, she had not cried that way for years. How nice that she could still feel things so deeply.

But Peter ignored Carol. "I think you're blowing things out of proportion," he told Jed. "And I don't want you bringing this up with your mom." An edge had come into his voice, and he paused for a moment. Barbara could see his back from where she crouched; it twitched almost imperceptibly. When Peter spoke again his tone was neutral. "Sometimes it's better just to let things pass, to let them resolve themselves on their own. If you talked to her you might—"

"Might what, Dad?" Jed demanded. "I don't understand. Might what?"

"Leave it alone, Jed," Peter said harshly. "You're too young to understand the damage you might do." He turned away abruptly and stared out into the hall. Barbara was sure he had sensed her presence—he was looking straight at her. She cringed a little farther into the darkness. Then she saw that his eyes were focused inward. As she watched, his facial muscles began to work crazily, convulsively, and for a moment it looked as if he were about to cry. Then his features congealed into a rictus of pain and woe.

Barbara knew that for this moment, at least, he saw it all—that with their life stripped for this brief time of all its custom he was forced to see it: the dry boneyard of their existence. Pleasure coursed through her like a river breaking onto a parched plain. It swelled her, and she luxuriated. And in this moment of fulfillment she knew: this was what she had wanted. This was what the pig was for.

Yet even as she exulted, Peter's expression was changing again. Fascinated, she watched him as slowly and with great effort he forced his features back into their normal aspect of impenetrable calm. He turned back to the children. "Listen to me, both of you. Carol, stop your crying now. We will have to be very kind to your mother." He spoke slowly, deliberately. "Very kind for a long, long time."

Sensing that the conference was close to an end, Barbara slipped down the dark hallway, back to her bed. She closed her eyes, feigning sleep, and it engulfed her, closing over her like the dark waters of the sea.

The next morning, the pig's head was gone. One by one the family ventured tentatively into the kitchen, to be greeted by the sight of Barbara on her knees, scrubbing out the refrigerator. Air freshener spread its artificial comfort; homemade Belgian waffles warmed in the oven.

Peter, concerned that the head might draw ants, slipped out to the trash bins behind the garage to see that it was properly wrapped. But there was no sign of the pig. It did not occur to him to search the yard. There, deep behind the rhododendrons that marked the farthest reaches of their property, he might have seen a mound of freshly turned earth, the Larousse laid upon it like a tombstone.

For a while, things improved. Barbara felt herself at the very center of her family, as she had been when the children were infants. There was a strained quality to Peter's concern, and to the children's attempts to include her in their lives, but Barbara did not mind, knowing as she did how conscious effort could grow in time into habit.

But then, in the way that families have, they abandoned their efforts, drifting slowly back to the patterns they were accustomed to. Barbara could feel their relief as they reverted. She tried to insert herself into their conversations and their plans, but she had become invisible again, inaudible. And the triumph she had felt the night of the family conference was lost to her.

One afternoon Carol came home and found her mother absent. Everything else was as it should be, but it was disturbing that there was no note, no explanation. Barbara had not returned by the time Peter came home from work, nor when Jed banged his way in the back door. No smell of dinner rose to meet them, and they wandered the house edgily, murmuring to one another.

At last, around 7:30, Barbara's car pulled into the driveway. "I can't believe how late it is," she sang as she entered the kitchen. Her voice, unnaturally cheery, drew them into the room.

"Let me help you with those," Jed offered, indicating the collection of Ralphs' bags around her knees. They were jammed with food.

"Oh, that's all right. They're not that heavy." With a protective gesture, and grinning a little crazily, Barbara stepped in front of the bags. "Just look at the time! If everyone will clear out and give me some room, I'll get dinner going. It's something we haven't had for a while. Something Spanish."

Efficiently, Barbara lifted the bags to the counter. No one else moved. They watched as if hypnotized as Barbara unloaded groceries: bright tomatoes; smooth, golden onions; a green profusion of limes, cilantro, and jalapeno. Then, what they were waiting for—a large package wrapped in butcher paper.

She unwrapped it slowly, eyeing them provocatively, and lifting the bundle of whitish flesh to her nose, she inhaled deeply. "Lovely!" she exclaimed. "The freshest snapper Ralphs has had in ages. You all liked snapper soup the last time I made it, didn't you?"

And she began to laugh. Oh, it was a terrible sound— she knew it was terrible. Her family's faces, horror-struck, confirmed it. Still, she could not stop. Wave after wave of hysterics assailed her until at last her knees buckled and she dropped unceremoniously to the floor. This set her off even more. Her throat ached from howling and her ribs felt as if they might crack.

The children were backing away from her, aghast, but Peter edged in closer, the expression on his face, all twisted again as it had been that other time, too comical to bear. She choked a bit, recovered, and then, unexpectedly, hiccupped. The laughter that this inspired nearly did her in. She rocked back and forth on the linoleum, red-faced and tear-stained and heaving helplessly. And as she rocked she wondered, with that small part of her brain still rooted to consciousness, if she would ever be able to stop.

Mrs. Santa Decides to Move
to Florida

April Selley

She doesn't remember a time when
she was anywhere except the North Pole
and believes that she truly did
spring from the head of legend.
There was no girlhood among grasses,
no dainty summer dresses.
She has always been married to a man over sixty
and wonders what it would be like
to put her arms around a boy
with no soft flesh.
She bakes—sweet things—
but no food is needed by immortals.
No one gets sick here or loses
a finger to a bandsaw.
The reindeer do not need litter boxes
or their coats brushed. There will be no children.
The androgynous elves craft a few toys,
but mostly get in shipments from Hong Kong.
Their laughter resonates for miles over the snow.
She hears it whenever she walks away.
She wonders,
if she walks far enough,
if time will begin for her,
if her eyelashes will freeze,
her eyeballs hurt in the -100° cold.
She wonders what the others would do
if they suddenly found her,
like a pillar of salt,
immobilized against the packed white.

The Weight of Me

Kristin Kearns
24:1 (2007)

My boyfriend is not the man he once was. A month ago he was twenty-six, ironing his shirts before work, proposing at dinner; a week later he was skinny and restless, smoking the cigarettes he'd quit before we met. Today I woke up to find him curled beside me, holding onto my earlobe with a hand half the size of mine. Now he is in the kitchen, trying to ride the cat.

I have dressed him in his boxer briefs, safety pinned at the waist to hide his shrinking penis. "Jonah," I tell him, "you're going to crush the cat."

He looks up at me with a smile that reminds me of him. "It likes it," he says, grabbing its tail.

Saint Bartholomew hunches his shoulders and blinks wearily at me. We found him as a kitten, abandoned in a box in the park. He accepts everything with resignation, as though awaiting his eternal reward. Our martyr cat.

Today Jonah seems to be about three years old, although I've never been good with ages, and it only becomes harder the younger he gets. At this rate he will be unborn by his birthday. I have made reservations at a Greek restaurant with singing waiters, the kind of place he finds embarrassing, not for himself but for the waiters. I have bought him another bottle of wine for his collection and a prize-winning board game that involves arranging tiles to form roads and cities and has an age rating of twelve plus. He likes this sort of game. He takes it very seriously, the claiming of territory, the strategic placement of cardboard squares.

I make Jonah a tuna fish sandwich and he hurls it at the wall. The bread sticks, held in place by mayonnaise and bits of Starkist. Jonah, my great love, an accountant with two degrees and his eye on some prize I've never been able to see, dances around the kitchen chanting, "Yucky yucky bo bucky banana fana fo fucky." He stubs his toe on the table leg and starts to cry.

"Grow up," I say, looking around for something to make him stop. I give him a cigarette, but he steps on it. I give him a spoon and he flings it to the floor with a clatter. Nothing stays in his hands anymore. I can't shake the feeling that his parents will come in at any moment and see the chaos, give me ten dollars, and drive me home in shuddering silence, as if I were a disaster barely averted.

At last I hold out a legal pad and a pen, and his sobs subside. "This isn't funny," I tell him. "I want my life back."

"Mine," he says, grabbing the Bic. I've about had it with him. He's been horrible since he stopped speaking in complete sentences. "Do you think this makes me want to marry you?" I say, but he isn't listening. He has climbed onto a chair and is drawing self-righteously, as if he belongs here, in this kitchen, in that little body.

He proposed on the last night of his forward development. He'd been talking about marriage since his younger brother got engaged to a woman he'd known for a month. He brought it up at odd times. For instance, one day I was rummaging through the dirty laundry for a shirt and he threw in a sock and said, "When we're married, we can open a joint account for furniture and groceries." I ruffled his curly head, patted his hopeful face, said, "That's good, sweetie pie." My mind wasn't on him. It was on the five years' worth of men I'd never met or kissed or fucked because of him. Suddenly and constantly they filled my head, and it made me sad, how many chances I'd missed. I began to feel very old and experienced and distant with all these men in my head. I drifted to the edge of the bed at night, away from Jonah, only one man and no longer enough, and he would wake and scoot closer.

"Come back," he'd say, nuzzling his head into the place between my neck and shoulder. After his runs, he flexed his thighs and made me feel: "See?" he said. "I'm strong." When he wanted to make love, he rubbed against me and said, "Can we do it? Can we?"

But he didn't want to do it that last night. After he'd proposed (don't be silly, baby, I said, nudging the ring away), he stood in the chilly backyard, holding an unlit cigarette and looking at the sky. He said, "This morning I woke up happy. I woke up thinking I'd already asked, and you'd said yes." I slipped my arms around him, placed my breasts against his back, tried to feel what I was letting go. He stooped under the weight of me.

"I'm sorry," I said. My heart thumped, mashed against my chest. He turned to face me, and his eyes were as dark as the sky. When I looked into them, it was like looking straight through his head. "Am I going to lose you?" he said.

"Not necessarily," I said. "Not right now."

He covered his face with my hand. I traced his eyebrows, his cheeks, his crooked nose, broken during a company baseball game a couple years back. I might never know another face so well.

"When?" he whined. I felt his damp lashes against my palm. "Next year? Tomorrow?"

I didn't know. I told him I didn't know anymore. I said, "Hang on, I'll ask god for a projected timeline of the rest of our lives."

"There is no rest of my life without you."

"Yes there is," I said, and felt as though I'd already left.

"No!" He pulled away and stomped on the wet grass, pulling at his hair. "It's not fair!" he said, his voice too loud. This isn't supposed to happen!" I watched him. I thought: I have no use for tantrums. But then he stopped. He dropped his arms and looked at me with ink-pooled eyes, and I saw how real he was, and how male, and how certainly he wanted me—more certainly than I'd ever wanted anything. "I wanted to grow old together," he said. "I guess we're growing apart instead."

I put my arms around him, but he was a sideways U straining away. He went inside and curled up on the edge of the bed, but in the morning he was spread on his back, arms and legs flung out. He woke up and smiled at the ceiling, and took his time looking in my direction. When he did he said, "For a second I thought you'd already gone."

"Not me," I said, surprised at how new he looked in the morning light.

The first few days I thought he was pulling away emotionally. But when his nose went suddenly straight, I understood that it was more than that. He opened one of his bottles of wine and instead of going to work, we made love, real love, desperate and hard like we didn't know each other. When I got up to shower, I turned and looked at him, and in that sex-flushed, straight-nosed face I saw the years ahead of us. His semen ran down my leg and my skin danced with his touch and five years together was nothing; I wanted six, seven, ten, even. In the bathroom I glanced in the mirror to see if my two-year-old scar had vanished from my chin. It hadn't. I looked into my eyes. If anything I looked older.

Now the man I almost married—didn't almost marry—may never marry—is drawing at the kitchen table, mad ballpoint squiggles. I keep my back to him as I clean tuna off the wall. The phone rings but I've stopped answering: It could be work, a friend, Jonah's parents, wanting some information I don't have, some conversation I can't summon. My vocabulary has diminished along with Jonah's.

The phone breaks off mid-ring, and before I can stop him, Jonah is holding the receiver with both hands. "Hello," he says, and listens. "No," he says. "No."

I grab the phone out of his hands. He slaps my leg. It is his mother; her voice is hard and she wants to know why a child is answering our phone. I say, "I'm practicing for my future with your son."

She goes silent. She says, "I was under the impression you didn't have one."

Jonah crumples a page from his legal pad and throws it at Saint Bartholomew, who is worming around my leg. I want to ask her what to do with a child who ought to be a man; she is a mother; mothers know things. Instead I tell her this isn't a good time.

"I was calling to leave a message for my son. I prefer to call him directly on his cell, but his voice mailbox is full." I have kept Jonah's phone on, hoping its ring will bring him back. NOT ENOUGH MEMORY has been flashing on the screen for days, and still it rings. I wonder where the cutoff is—when people decide you are not coming back, how long before they write you off.

His mother wants to know whether Jonah has booked his flight for his brother's wedding. "We haven't," I say, emphasizing the we. I tell her we have to check our options.

"You're turning twenty-seven this year, aren't you?" For no reason I can see, Jonah starts yelling.

"Yes." I stick my finger in my free ear. "November thirteenth."

"By the time I was twenty-two, I was married with two children," she says. "Women peak earlier than men, you know. I'm curious, how many options do you think you have?"

Jonah yells again. I hang up the phone and yell back at him as loud as I can, blood rushing to my head. He looks surprised and stops, but I keep going. It feels good to yell like this, without saying anything. I could knock him over with my breath. He throws his Bic at me and runs out of the kitchen, his boxer briefs sagging. There he goes: my best option.

My best option wets the bed overnight. In the morning my best option wets his pants and after he eats there is shit on the chair. He sits in his shit and cries and this is when I know: This is it; I can't take it anymore. I cannot watch my certain, strong-thighed, sky-eyed man losing control of his body like an old man who has lived too long.

I dress him in my shirt, and on the way to the emergency

room relief settles on me. They will tell me what's wrong. That is their job.

He sits on a metal chair beside me and cries; the other people glare at us as if we're in a movie theater instead of a hospital. None of them looks at all sick or hurt, just tired and uncomfortable. One woman is leaning her head on a man's shoulder, the way I used to with Jonah, when he was the right height.

In the blue-curtained examining room the doctor hoists Jonah up on the table, looks him over and says, "Well, here's your problem." At once the fluorescent-lit room grows ten watts brighter. My heart beats so quickly I can hardly feel it and I think: Thank god. Thank god for doctors, for science, for this world in which nothing is unknown. I wait for the doctor to give Jonah a shot, a pill, a prescription for himself.

"How long has he been out of diapers?" the doctor asks.

"Diapers?"

He pins Jonah into a clean white cloth and, without asking, dumps the boxer briefs into the trash. Jonah stops crying. The doctor holds a stethoscope to his chest.

"That's all it is?"

The doctor doesn't speak. He seems angry with me. He shines a light into Jonah's ears and eyes and mouth, and I keep waiting for him to look at me and say, "This is no baby, Ms. Keene. There's a man in here." Finally he lifts Jonah off the table, writes "Huggies" on a piece of paper, and hands it to me. "If you run to the emergency room every time he has a bowel movement, he's going to grow up afraid of his own body."

He reaches into a jar on the counter and pulls out a lollipop. I want to tell him Jonah's not going to grow up at all. I want to tell him that I'm afraid of his own body. I tell him, "He doesn't like lollipops." But Jonah has taken off the wrapper and is happily sucking. I lead him out, betrayed. It seems a vital piece of information, this former affinity for hard lickable candy, something I should have known before I considered spending any part of my life with him.

"What else haven't you told me?" I ask as I buckle him into the back seat. He smacks me with the lollipop and it sticks to my face. I get into the car and back out of the parking space, the warm wetness of the lol¬lipop both creepy and comforting, like someone who loves you whom you don't love back.

In the morning I take him out of bed, and instead of standing he falls to his knees, his limbs turned to rubber. I create a fence of pillows and shut Saint Bartholomew out of the bedroom. I have heard that cats suck babies' breath. I grind food in the blender, spaghetti, omelets, foods he used to eat whole when he had teeth. I try not to see the mashed shredded wheat streaking his face; I look hard into my mind until I see him as he was, the hair trailing down his chest, the way he held his arms just the slightest bit away from his sides when he wanted a hug, like he wasn't sure I'd give it. I think of him this way because I believe that any day now time will right itself, pull him along until my body fits again into his. I am waiting for the catch-up, the convergence, the moment when he comes up to meet me like a swimmer for air.

It will happen like this: I will go for a long walk and I will not think of him, and when I return he will be waiting for me, his legs going for miles beneath his boxer briefs. Let's start over, he'll say, and together we will. I go for this walk while he naps, and then I sit in the living room, building the courage to check on him.

When I do, I find that his diaper is wet.

I squint as I diaper him, to keep from seeing his tiny penis, floppy and no bigger than my thumb. I remember the way it swelled and fit inside me. "Baby," he called me, "my girl." Now it sends out a squirt of urine onto my neck and he smiles. "Pee," he says, and I start to cry.

He used to put his hand on my stomach as if I were growing, gestating, my body filling with some invisible force. I miss this. I want a ring on my finger that I can bite when I miss things too much. I have looked for the ring he proposed with, but it's not in the pocket of the jacket he wore that night. It is not in his desk or in any of the dresser drawers or in his soft leather briefcase. I am afraid he swallowed it or flushed it down the toilet. I am afraid he proposed to a toddler at the playground where I took him last week when I was feeling guilty of depriving him of youth. One day I will see a three-year-old in the canned foods aisle with my ring swimming on her finger, and I will hate her for what she has: a four-thousand-dollar piece of him, wearable, losable, clear as running water. "Mine," I'll say, and grab for it.

I put him to sleep in our bed and lie on the couch to keep from crushing him, but I can't sleep. I walk into the night-dampened yard and hold my breasts, pretend that my hands are his back and my breasts are his face, that I can feel all of him at once, and all of me as well.

Tomorrow is his birthday. I will it not to come, despite the game gift-wrapped and waiting in the closet. I do not fancy waking to find him covered in blood, crying, his eyes not yet open. I will have to wrap him in a blanket and wait for him to shrink away. Because he is not a cat, I can't leave him in a box in the bushes.

And then? And then I don't know. Maybe his mother will look down to find herself pregnant again.

Inside the house he is surrounded by pillows, clutching the stuffed lamb that he used to make dance. I take his hand. It disappears into mine and he wakes up, blinks, his skin warm, smooth from sleep like an ocean-polished rock. He has always looked this way when he wakes: a little boy, unhurried as curtains in a breeze. We would have been so much happier if he could always be just waking.

I lie down and curl myself around him while I still can. I wonder if he will be born again, and if he will grow at this new, increased speed. I wonder if he will live the same life, if he will meet me again; and if so, I wonder how old

I will be and whether he will remember me, or at least see me the way he once did.

Crow Mercies

Penelope Scambly Schott
Crow Mercies (2010)

—in memory of Marian Schott 1919-2009

The Art of the Poetic Line
   High on a wire:
   clothespins or crows

Farewell to the Old Days
   When we were young and beautiful,
   when we were fools

What We Thought Then
   That someone would jump in to save us,
   that you never forget how to ride a bike

Wisdom
   One-who-knew met One-who-didn't-know,
   and it was hard to know the differences

Tyrannies of the Bedspread
   My mother, too old and sick
   to spy it folded up on the chair

Fragility
   The top curve of her left ear
   parting her limp hair

Marriage
   I told my husband,
   If you die, I'll kill you

Sexual Dimorphism after Sixty

Long, thick hair in his nose and ears,
sparse or non in her groin

Who Remembers Least?
    Humans, crows, ladybugs, ferns, algae,
    Shoes, toasters, doorsteps, invisible ink?

Jet Set
    My mother traveled by air;
    now crow flies without her

Party Decorations
    When the goldfinches show up,
    poppies bobble yellow petals

Botheration
    A flock of common grackles conquers
    the bird feeder; even crow surrenders

Mercy
    Clothespins on socks
    or a string on a crow's foot

High Fashion
    So like a wood duck, elegant in dress
    though she spoke with the voice of a crow

Ars Poetica
    As a rule, I do not sell my dreams;
    as a rule, I break rules

Flock
    The clothes on the line
    flapped while wings

Recalculating

Jennifer Burd
28:3 (2015)

My mother can't draw us a map,
but the short distance between
her grandmothers' houses
is still in her body.

The GPS instructs as we drive
through the town where she grew up.
She speaks of the past as a single address,
remembering each number nailed

on the house where she first
kissed my father and learned
to keep secrets from her sister.
It's what I've just said that hides,

darting behind cloud, leaf, or door,
a dream from which she is always
waking up and trying to remember.
But the long-lived still flexes

in her muscles as she ignores
the digital voice that tells
what to do, in how many feet.
As in our childhood games,

we get closer, grow warmer,
and I try to anticipate where
I will turn in a future in which
my mother doesn't know who I am.

The unit can always figure

another way, wherever we are,
but only after the street names
Vaughn, White, Granger roll off

my mother's tongue do we arrive.
Now, parked in front of the 1940s
memories of the grandmother
who painted roses on blank china,

my mother knows where to go:
"It's walking distance
to my other grandmother's"—
the one who could bake light

loaves of bread without tools
to measure—and she gets us there,
but can't for the life of her
tell us how to get back home.

I BELIEVE
I AM BEGINNING
Our Place With The Universe

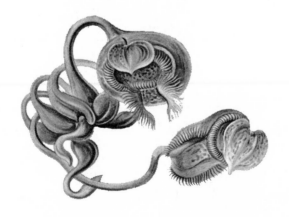

As human beings we seek to create order in our world; we develop a long sight, meditate on the human condition, and find a niche to tuck, saint-like, into. For some this niche becomes a place of certainty; for others, it raises more questions; but still we fly, moth-like, toward the flame of belonging. We seek it in organized religion, in communion with nature, and in connection with our histories. These works address culture, history, spirituality, nature, and our relationship with each.

The exclusion of women's voices from most of the history of philosophy, history, and culture has led, throughout the centuries, to the development of a unique relationship with the sublime. Long associated with the "earthly" pleasures, women were considered by many to be incapable of grasping concepts beyond debased drudgery. As women have worked to reclaim our right to the divine, and to resist the racialized and gendered personifications we are presented, our stories become the stories of humanity: of release, and of triumphant reclaiming. Here we see the claiming of texts and traditional religions that have been banned, works of powerful love and loss, and works of the heart as well as the soul. Some are a literal return to religion, some are the finding of the divine in ourselves, and all represent the power of the human spirit.

Relics

Barbara Garden Baldwin
1:1 (1976)

There are ladders
in the sky, starry skeletons.
I stand on my lover's
shoulders and climb. Heaven

is an empty belly,
mother, the hope of lonely
men. God is love
painted gold on Sunday,

my bones another rung
for Jacob's clan. The world
disappears inside my
eyes, the cobalt cry of space

unwinds. My head crowds
the stars, beneath my feet
a blue infinity
I believe I am beginning

to understand silence
and recurring echoes. The logical
consistency of water
erases us. Give me your hand.

I am small enough
to sleep curled in your palm,
talisman of your
cautious courage, totem of bone.

Remember the Moon Survives

Barbara Kingsolver
9:1 (1985)

—for Pamela

Remember the moon survives,
draws herself out crescent-thin,
a curved woman. Untouchable,
she bends around the shadow
that pushes itself against her, and she

waits. Remember how you waited
when the nights bled their darkness out
like ink, to blacken the days beyond,
to blind morning's one eye.
This is how you learned to draw
your life out like the moon,
curled like a fetus around the

shadow. Curled in your bed,
the little hopeful flowers of your knees
pressed against the wall
and its mockery of paint,
always the little-girl colors
on the stones of the ordinary prison:
the house where you are someone's
daughter, sister, someone's flesh, someone's

blood. The Lamb and Mary
have left you to float in this darkness
like a soup bone. You watch
the cannibal feast from a hidden place
and pray to be rid of your offering.
The sun is all you wait for,

the light, guardian saint of all the children
who lie like death on the wake

of the household crime. You stop
are not your own. You hide
your life away, the lucky coin
tucked quickly in the shoe
from the burglar, when he

comes. Because he will, as sure
as shoes. This is the one
with all the keys to where you live,
the one you can't escape, and while
your heart is stopped, he takes things.
It will take you years

to learn: why you hold back sleep
from the mouth that opens in the dark;
why you will not feed it with
the dreams you sealed up tight
in a cave of tears; why
the black widow stills visits you,
squeezes her venom out in droplets,
stringing them like garnets
down your abdomen,
the terrifying jewelry of a woman
you wore inside, a child robbed

in the dark. Finally you know this.
You have sliced your numbness open
with the blades of your own eyes.
From your years of watching
you have grown the pupils of a cat, to see

in the dark. And these eyes are
your blessing. They will always know
the poison from the jewels that are both

embedded in your flesh.
They will always know the darkness
that is one of your names by now,
but not the one you answer to.
You are the one who knows, behind
the rising, falling tide
of shadow, the moon is always

whole. You take in silver
through your eyes, and hammer it
as taut as poems in steel
into the fine bright crescent of your life:
the sickle,
the fetus,
the surviving moon.

Gravity Reversed

Frances Payne Adler
Raising the Tents (1993)

—for Sybil

On the day gravity is reversed,
pots that hang from the kitchen ceiling
turn upright and fill themselves
with everything I ever cooked.
Chairs repeat exact conversations of table talk.

Even the clocks are affected,
roll backwards. Photo albums
lining the living room walls
turn upright the years since my birth,
click my mother back to life.
She climbs down from bookshelves,
dressed in summer cotton,
looks in pots for something to eat.

She fills the halls,
different aged versions of herself.
Twenty-four at the piano, in satin, in love.
Forty in the flowered chair
watching through windows.
Fifty-nine writing at her desk.
Black has slipped from her hair
to pockets under her eyes.

There are some things
even gravity can't unloose.
Momma, I say, *talk to me.*
She smiles for the camera.
I bend over her, watch her write.

Nā Wāhine Noa

Haunani-Kay Trask
Light in the Crevice Never Seen (1994)

Rise up, woman gods.
Have Hina as your goddess
virgin, volcanic
unto herself.

Without masters, marriages
lying parasite men.
Unto her self:
a wise eroticism

moondrawn by the tides
culling love
from great gestating Pō
massive night

birthing women's dreams:
magma bodies
flowing volcanoes
toward moonred skies.

The title Nā Wāhine Noa means "free women" in the sense of those released from the restrictive Hawaiian system of kapu (taboo) where, among other divisions and proscriptions, the genders were separated and women were considered defiling.

Hina—the goddess of the moon—is a woman who beats kapa—bark cloth used for traditional clothing—in the night sky. She is a woman free of husbands and other men because she has escaped to the heavens.

Life Is A Dance

Mary Cuffe Perez
The Woman of Too Many Days (1999)

Life is a dance, says the woman of too many days.

She's shelling peanuts on the corner of Lark and
Washington.
The pigeons peck at the shells impatiently.
How the woman of too many days eats peanuts without
teeth I don't know,
but there 's sure nothing but shells coming down to the
pigeons.

You got to take that life comin up in you
and give it a shape.
Sometimes it comes on like a river,
pushin everything back
like the world was just furniture
in its way.

Sometimes you got to tap it out
hard and sharp, or you got to twist it
into something new move
you're just learning how to do.

And sometimes you just let it lay you out,
wide and quiet.
Then you give it a toss of your hip
and your dancin another dance.

Not everybody knows the dance.
Those that do, don't know they do.
They're just steppin to the rhythm that olays
through their tie, goes with their step.

I can tell a dancer.
Even if they're waitin for the bus,
even if they're sittin with their head down.
hands hangin between their knees,
even if they forgot the music and all the words,
even if their body's broke down.

A dancer is always a dancer.

hey are shaped to the dance
like the land that will hold the shape of a river
gone through.
Like the rails of a train sing
with the train gone by.

Like a jig in the laugh when the feet don't move.

I can tell a dancer.

And the Eyes of the Blind
Shall Be Opened

Elizabeth McLagan
20:1 (2001)

It's all I can do not to stray from the high
holy Latin to the risen Christ, flanked by disciples,
ascended, or are they descending above the altar,
above the anorexic Jesus racked to the cross.

This scene like a mediation of things to come,
between the bells and candles and incense
of my blind faith, but it's not the resurrected face
I contemplate so much as the drape of cloth

that billows about Him like a pregnancy.
And I worry about the way His feet flap below
the ankles like the feet of a hanged man or my own
when I hung on the school yard monkey bars

mouthing all the dirty words I knew.
I remember our Baptist pastor, his gap-toothed grin
and mousy exhausted wife, the evidence
of their sexual life stair-stepping the front pew.

Our bodies were empty vessels, he said, and I thought
of my mother's milk-glass pitcher, hobnailed
with small, aggressive breasts, and of my own body,
tipped
so the flames could drain from my eyes, my mouth,

the tips of my fingers. And Jesus would fill me
as mist pours into trees or ice numbs my mouth
until my words would slur into ecstasy. Even now

it's not that I wouldn't want to be one of the disciples,

ascend the strung-out laundry of sky, let the wind
bend my back into a curve and be filled
with something that swells with the light
to come. *She*, I still whisper, when we name

the Holy Spirit, though it's harder to follow
the Latin mutter. There's a moth somewhere, wakened
from darkness. I feel it flutter against me, against
the bright weight of all I am not supposed to say.

Making Do: A Fable

Sarah Lantz
Far Beyond Triage (2007)

—for Laurena Marrone

By October the numbers had become catastrophic¬
words vanishing without a trace—
dead or disappeared went the word
for the sag of a skiff abandoned
at its dock-side mooring;
gone was the word for wool spun from a brown lamb
startled twice by an August thunderclap.
Missing was a word similar to "miasma"
but bigger, a word for an entire culture
when it has lost its vision.
That was only the beginning.

Some words became sick—
was "tender" a term for meat or money?
Was "piccolo" an instrument, a beloved,
or a word that simply meant small?
Only a "ga" sound remained
of the word uttered when the twitch of a scup
nibbling on a line gives way to a strike.
Following the fate of canaries in mines,
koala bears, and other telltale species,
poets began to malinger.

From White Space to Black Letter:
Taking My Place
in the Women's Torah

Ada Molinoff
27:3 (2013)

"To be a Jew means to tell my story within the Jewish story."
—*Rabbi Laura Geller*

As I picked up the October 2010 issue of my synagogue newsletter, an announcement for the Women's Torah Project caught my attention. The completion of the first Torah inscribed by a collaborative group of women was being celebrated, and the public was invited the next week to the University of Washington's Hillel Center in Seattle, just two hundred miles north. The schedule included "Sewing Together Torah Panels." Not only had they refused to accept the prohibition against women "writing Torah"— they were actually going to assemble the scroll. I felt pulled to join them by an invisible thread.

On the train, I thought about the *Rosh Hashanah* when I was fourteen. My mother, brought up Socialist, didn't believe in organized religion and wouldn't be attending services for the Jewish New Year. I approached my father as he knotted his tie.

"I'll go to temple with you," I'd said.

"Really?" he asked, his eyebrows arching. "Good!"

I wouldn't understand the service because I'd had no Hebrew lessons. I hadn't become a *bat mitzvah* because there was no such ceremony in the Orthodox Judaism in which my father had been raised. But I relished our chat as we drove in the Buick the five miles to the next town. I also stayed busy tugging my new straight skirt over my unfamiliar nylon stockings, squirming to tuck in my blouse, and corralling wisps of my dark hair into the band that held my ponytail. When we arrived, I carefully stepped from the car on patent leather heels to follow my father into the small white building.

No one had told me about the women's balcony.

"Dad, can't I sit with you?" I asked, apprehension leaking into my voice.

"No. You have to go up there. I'll wait for you afterward, outside."

I squeezed onto a hard bench where the only available space was between two large women who pressed against my shoulders. Their "perspiration," in the polite diction of 1960, tracked down their powdered and rouged cheeks in the early September heat. I peered over the railing to search the red-plush pews for my father, found him at the end of a crowded row, raising his hand in his yearly pledge. I watched as the men took their turns reading aloud from the Torah. *Not a man, not Jewish enough* looped through my mind.

In Seattle, inside the foyer at the Hillel Center, a sign pointed to the second floor. I took the steps slowly. Upstairs, double doors had been thrown open to reveal a large room with shifted furniture where women in twos and threes leaned over their tasks.

My body hummed like a high-voltage wire but I stood stock-still. "*Closer,*" said a voice within me. I walked in.

Sunlight flooded the room from a dozen windows and light wood flooring honeyed the air. The peaked ceiling in hues of desert sand and red earth echoed the tent of Sarah and Abraham. Stacks of creamy parchment inscribed with the crisp outlines of Hebrew script, the black ink so new it shined, covered every surface.

In respect for an open Torah, I clipped on my *kippah*, though I felt shy whenever I wore a skullcap. I shrugged off uneasiness to approach a woman who stood in the center of the room. Her face was open and she was short like me so we looked eye to eye. She introduced herself as Linda from New Jersey, one of the scribes. She wore a poncho-like daily prayer shawl, its trailing fringes grazing the table as she pushed aside small rolls of parchment curled by their carrying tubes. She spread a panel, anchored its corners with weights wrapped in white tissue paper. When she touched the panel, the weights looked close to falling off.

"Can I help you?"

"Do you read Hebrew?" she asked, looking up.

"No, I've forgotten it. I'm sorry," I said to the top of Linda's head. Having heard the beginning of my answer, she'd returned to verifying that her inscriptions matched the Torah's text. *Not Jewish enough* stabbed through me.

I felt like I did when I was twenty-six, at Chanukah, when I hadn't known there were prayers to be said over a menorah I didn't yet own. On the eighth and final afternoon of the Festival of Lights, while the late-day sun slanted through my apartment, I'd stood a candle I saved for special occasions on the white enamel stovetop between the black burners. I struck a match and moved it toward the wick.

The candle fell over. I shook out the match, rummaged for aluminum foil, wadded it in my fist, poked my finger in the middle to make a holder, and stuck in the candle. Again it wouldn't stand. I grabbed the candle, shoved it in a drawer. *Not enough* rose in me like acrid smoke. Back then, I hadn't known how to be Jewish.

My attention returned to the Project when Linda struggled to flatten another sheet of Torah. She worked bare-handed, contrary to Jewish custom. We're taught not to touch a Torah, so the oil from our fingers won't mar its surface. White cotton gloves, like museum curators use, lay on one end of the table. "I tried to wear them," she said. "They got in the way."

I reached out, held the panel in place. I thrilled to

the touch of parchment as my fingers grasped the sharp corners of every piece.

A few feet away stood Hannah, an Israeli scribe, who flipped two panels of Torah onto a table that had been covered by brown wrapping paper to protect her inscriptions. The underside of the parchment swirled with the shadowy patterns of cowhide.

She grasped two sheets and bent their ends into flaps that she placed against each other. Gripping a small awl in her fist, she pointed its metal tip at a spot along the seam and pushed. She worked the point to form holes then threaded beige sinew through a four-inch silver needle that she'd use to stitch the panels together. I swallowed my chagrin at having brought along an ordinary needle and thread, assuming they'd be useful. Hannah tied an end knot—"Just like sewing," she said.

Rachel, the scribe from Brazil, sewed Torah nearby. She handed the awl and needle to the woman beside her who soon looked to see who wanted to be next. "*Now,*" said my inner voice.

Feeling the heft of the tool against my palm, I leaned over until my cheek almost brushed the parchment.

"*Go ahead,*" said the voice.

I'll tear it.

"*You won't hurt it.*"

I pushed, pushed harder. The point pierced. Withdrawing it, I saw I'd created clean openings. I pulled at the needle, felt the sinew catch as it scratched through. *Done.* I looked up, smiled as I exhaled.

I moved to the doorway to collect myself and turned to the director of the Project.

"I was afraid I'd ruin it," I said, my voice soft.

"Oh," she said, looking at me in shared understanding.

"Damage was the old message," I said. "We've been afraid we'd injure the Torah, hurt Judaism." I shook my head. "We'll make it better." We nodded as if in time to the same *niggun* sung by our grandmothers.

Someone signaled the director to another part of the room as the bearded young rabbi from Hillel approached. They'd lent that space to the Project's congregation.

Our silence grew awkward and I looked for a way to break it.

"Isn't this amazing?" I asked.

"Yes," he answered, "it's huge. Much bigger than the attention it's getting. Women have been in the white spaces and now they're in the black letters. I have a six-month-old daughter and her experience of Judaism is going to be so different from my mother's, whose father was a rabbi. My mother told me she couldn't go near the Torah." As he left, I guessed his mother and I would have been about the same age.

I recalled the year I was fifteen, the time I decided to wear a Star of David at Passover dinner. I'd felt a jolt of excitement as I fastened the necklace around my neck and checked it in the mirror. When we arrived at Aunt Bea's, I followed the aroma of pot roast to the kitchen. She hugged me, then held me at arm's length to look at my necklace. Her face hardened as she told me the family didn't like it when people wore crosses—or stars. "We know you're Jewish," she said.

My embarrassment burned as I clasped my hand over the pendant. I wanted to disappear.

During the *seder* I dug down, retrieved the feeling that had led me to put on the star. I shut my eyes tight, wishing, wishing to feel . . . something. I wanted to believe, to belong, not only because my family was Jewish—I wanted to *feel* Jewish. But wearing that necklace had broken my family's unspoken rule against *acting* Jewish.

I had been born right after World War II. The Holocaust haunted our home. My parents discussed Jewish matters in low tones, and only within the extended family, as if to build a wall around our religion. They were afraid for me to stand out as a Jew. In the hush of their worry, and in Aunt Bea's reaction to my necklace, I heard the message,

"Don't be too Jewish." I put away the star and retreated to the margins to watch others practice Judaism, convinced it was the wrong thing for me to want.

After I left home, I sought religion in bits and pieces, studied as if I were stringing pearls. I wouldn't risk more until middle age, when I learned the Hebrew alphabet from a programmed workbook, preparing for my *bat mitzvah*.

One day the rabbi and I met for lunch.

"What do I do about a Hebrew name?" I asked, my eyes fixed on my plate. "I wasn't given one at birth."

She smiled. "You choose your own name."

"I've always liked the name Miriam," I said, almost whispering.

"Miriam it is. Miriam you are."

I felt as if a new self had been born.

By the time of my trip to Seattle fifteen years after my *bat mitzvah*, my Jewish education had become occasional. But now, as a Project committee member told me that archaeologists in Israel had unearthed rocks with women's prayers on them, I wanted more regular study. The Women's Torah was adding to a stream of voices that had been flowing forward for millennia. I could almost see the room brighten while we spoke of those women from ancient times, their spirits, like light, arriving from the edge of our galaxy.

Moments later, a woman in her twenties walked through the room as if finding her way. I followed her gaze to Rachel stitching panels.

I stepped closer. "Would you like to sew some?" I asked.

"Can I? I thought they do that," she said, her chin pointing toward the scribes.

"It's for anyone. You could go over and watch and then you can do it."

"Oh," she said, her eyes wide. She sat next to Rachel to wait her turn in a new version of *l'dor va dor*—"from generation to generation."

The legacy my generation had inherited confronted me late that afternoon. I was touring the room's perimeter to admire ritual objects that artists had created and donated to the Project. There was a glass cup for the *Kiddush* blessing . . . inlaid rollers for the finished Torah. I stopped in front of the pointer. The artist had carved that *yad* in curves like bends in a river, so different from traditional ones that are ramrod-straight. I picked it up, felt it reverse the hurt of having been excluded because I was a girl, kept out by a Judaism that had been unyielding. The new pointer, its wood warm to my touch, fit my hand as if it had been made for me.

In writing the Women's Torah, the scribes had kept many traditions. They'd bestowed each letter with a prayerful intention, an imperceptible mist that bonded it to the sacred scroll. And, they'd written freehand, without stencils. For the ending celebration, they had left blank the final hundred letters, to fill in their penciled outlines as tributes and as fundraisers.

I handed over a small donation to a Project member. "This is in support of the Project, for a letter. And it's for all who couldn't attend," I said, my tears welling in longing for a letter of my own. I was giving it away because I still couldn't believe it was mine to have.

"No, no. It's for you too," she said, taking my check. "It will be *your* letter." I could only nod my gratitude.

I sought respite in the doorway. A tall young woman climbed the stairs lugging a video camera and gear, and as we chatted I learned she was filming a documentary about one of the scribes.

Later she asked if she could interview me. I expected to shake my head, but instead said, "Yes, I'll do it," and settled into a chair. Balancing the camera on her shoulder, she requested that I identify myself and tell why I was there and how I felt about it. She grinned encouragement.

"I was born into a Jewish family," I said to the lens, "but

I didn't receive a Jewish education until my *bat mitzvah* at age forty-eight. I'm sixty-four, and for women of my generation . . ." My face crumpled. I looked away, swallowed. "This Torah, made by women, is *very* important and this celebration feels *very* meaningful."

During dinner in my hotel room I reflected on why I'd been so moved. Slowly I understood why I nearly wept that afternoon while telling my story. I'd seen, as if for the first time, that I'd felt on my own untangling Judaism, a Gordian knot because of my era, my family, and my emotions. Being Jewish had been lonely.

The Project had drawn me in through wide open doors. I could be a woman and feel fully Jewish and I could act it—wear a *kippah*, sew Torah. Finally, I felt Jewish enough.

After dinner I walked back to the Project, the folds of my skirt flowing as if stirred by wind currents off the Negev. Linda had taken her place at a table that held the last panel of the Women's Torah. Each time someone approached her, she nodded permission, bent to her work. She finished scribing a letter for a woman in a shawl. "*Now*," sang my inner voice. I walked across the room, a distance that felt much greater than it was.

I'd come in from the white space.

"Would you do a letter for me?" I asked, my voice quavering with the fear of having breached a boundary I'd felt forbidden to cross.

"Of course," Linda said. "Stand here, beside me." She pointed her quill. "This final passage is about the death of Moses. Your letter is *pay*, the beginning of the word, *panim*, face. Moses was the first who met God face-to-face."

"Oh," I said, tears brimming.

"Put your hand lightly on mine," she said.

I rested my hand on hers, felt her skin soft beneath my fingers. Stroke by stroke we inked in the empty shape until my letter was dark as night, shiny as morning.

Home

Margarita Donnelly
28:2 (2015)

Three excerpts from "Swimming with Piranhas," an unfinished memoir, written both from the perspective of an adult and a child.

I.

It stands out like a dream. Perfect weather, not too hot, never cold. The daytime skies are clear and full of airy clouds against an azure blue. At night the stars shine brilliantly in a velvet black sky. The flowers are radiant and sweetly perfumed. The ocean is warm and aqua colored. The birds are brilliant and noisy with brassy voices that fill the air with song. The mountains are purple and majestic. The great vast *llanos* buzz with *chicharos* and surrealistic fauna. My life is filled with family and godparents. Everyone I know is loving and full of energy. In my memories and dreams my childhood was spent in paradise. And then I came north.

The North is a confusion, not of language, because I have been bilingual all my life, but of weather, of culture, of identity. Since I left Venezuela so suddenly, I have always been confused. And I never understood the ramifications of that confusion until I returned decades later.

When I came north, the memory of Venezuela and its landscape was a memory of light, of color, of warmth, of beauty, of roundness, softness, noise, music, and joy. The North was a country of angles, silences, grayness, fog, cold, darkness, and too many seasons. Seasons that I have never completely acclimatized to, that continue to catch me by surprise. My tongue grew up with the sweetness of the tropics, mango, *lechosa, chirimoya, guanabana, parchita, merey.*

The heavy texture of yucca and manioc. Of thick soups, *auyama* and *sancocho*, on the stoves of my godparents and in my own home as my mom learned the intricacies of cooking turtle and fish soups.

Spanish was the first language I spoke. The language of reality, romance, complexity, and lyricism. It formed in my mouth like music. It gurgled out like water. English was a language of harsh directness—a language of rectitude, non-melodic, spoken in the front of my mouth with little expression. Spanish emanated from a deep recess in my being, the mouth succulently forming and moving with its rhythmic cadence. A language in which poetry was spoken. Where singing could break out at any moment. Where everyday conversations were long and complex. English was economic, a sort of Morse code, the language of business and rules and direction. It formed a straight line encompassing angles; Spanish was a moving obliqueness encompassing passion.

The rhythm of the North was different, jangling with metallic sharpness—the music different, dancing different. The pace of life rapid, scheduled, regulated. Meals were strange, not just because of the bland food, but because they were so utilitarian and served at such odd hours. They were no longer the languid affairs of my childhood lasting for hours over animated discussions. Meals were served early and finished in short time spans. No two-hour lunches or ten-at-night suppers. Suppers at six felt like a *merienda* to me and are still too early. My circadian rhythm survives from a childhood of meals served late into the evening.

My mother had traveled by ship to Venezuela six months pregnant with me. She traveled to join my father with my brother who was three years old. Three days after her ship left New York City, Pearl Harbor was bombed and the ship she traveled on was the last passenger liner to cross the Caribbean until WWII ended. My two sisters were left behind in boarding school because my mother had to leave in a hurry—my father was sick. What should have been only a temporary separation lasted the duration of the war. I would not meet my sisters until the war was over.

My mother named me after Isla Margarita because I was her Venezuelan pearl. We lived in Caracas under the shadow of Mount Avila. Our first house was named by my parents *Quinta Palmasola*, for my mother the singer. I remember the slats of my crib and the safety I felt under the latched screening that kept the bugs out. My earliest memory is of a burglar stealing into my room and unlatching my crib. I was not scared, even when he stole my blanket. The burglar smiled at me and I laughed at him. Years later I would learn it was my father stealing the blanket I had gotten too attached to.

Music was all around me. It was the fabric of our lives. My father and his band practiced late into the night, my mother played the piano and sang during the day. She sang me to sleep at night with a lullaby and placed angels at my head, and at my side, and at the foot of my bed to guard and protect me all night long.

II.

The piano is tall. It is full of sound. Daddy sits there, his hands on the black and white keyboard. A song is singing from the keyboard. I go to his feet under the board. His feet go up and down hitting the floor making sounds. It is dark under there but Daddy's legs are moving. I crawl up between his legs. Daddy pulls me into his lap and I rock on his knees. Daddy's fingers go up and down the board pushing the black and white keys. He sings a song with the song of the piano. And I am jiggling on his knees and laughing. Daddy looks down and smiles at me. I put my hands on his arms and laugh with him as they move on those keys making the song. We are making a song, Daddy and I, on all those black and white keys. I help him push them down. Daddy moves fast, his fingers are quick, my hands are small and can't push as fast. But Daddy doesn't mind and laughs more as I help him push the keys. His chin moves up and down. I watch him from below. His moustache curls into a smile. He looks down at me. His eyes smile too and his hands move faster and I bounce on his knees bumping into the board and laughing. "Play the José song!" I say, and Daddy laughs louder. "Play kitten on the keys!" I say and his fingers move even faster and his knees change their jiggle and I can see the kitten playing on the black and white keys as my daddy laughs and I jiggle and the song gets louder and louder and daddy and I are rocking to the song of kittens playing on the black and white keys.

III.

For my fifty-fifth birthday I only wanted to visit my mother's grave. I had dutifully carried the instructions to find Mamma's grave that Daddy sent to all his children before he died. She is buried in the old cemetery on what used to be the edge of the urban sprawl against the Andean mountains of Caracas. Chepa, a friend, is taking me on a tour of my natal city after the birthday lunch of *lapa*. But we have not gone near the cemetery. I thought this time I would finally get my wish and visit Mama's grave. But it is too dangerous. Instead, on my fifty-fifth birthday, I am in Bolivar Plaza in the city where I was born. We have looked for my old neighborhood and I am not sure we even came close to *Quinta Erin*, my last home in Caracas before we moved to the *llanos* of Anzoategui.

A man is singing me a serenade and the cuatro is sounding the syncopated rhythm of the *joropo* with the maracas and the harp in counterpoint. He sings a dramatic *llanero* ballad in a high falsetto gesturing toward me. I am delighted and embarrassed at the same time. Chepa and I are being treated as the *llaneras* we are by the Caraqueños.

I don't remember the song but I know its intensity, the

rhythm, and the high piercing exclamations of passion. It is a part of me, a rhythm embedded in my being, as natural as breathing and walking. The singing is intense. The musicians don't know me and yet they find me and I find myself in this music. It knows me as it is a part of me. It is the old home we did not find and the grave I cannot visit and these rhythms anchor me, establishing a transition from that past into this present. I am standing in Bolivar Plaza surrounded by the rhythms of Venezuela, receiving a gift I could not have imagined. I feel the pulse of life, my life, the life my mother would have wanted me to live. And I am home in the city where I was born. I cannot visit my mother's grave—instead this ballad fills me with generosity, beauty, and yes, love.

About CALYX

Mimeograph; Blueline; Color plate: Terms that have become archaic in our digital publishing world—or at least have become nearly unrecognizable in the last four decades. Forty years have brought us track changes, digital proofs, and inset color pages, but they have lessened neither the need for a safe space for women's voices nor the commitment to the profoundly egalitarian and feminist ideals on which CALYX was founded.

Launched in 1976 by Margarita Donnelly, Barbara Baldwin, Elizabeth McLagan, and Meredith Jenkins, CALYX was a specialty women's press in the era of "kitchen table presses." Indeed, it is tempting to imagine these four pioneers sitting around a cozy table deciding to publish a little literary magazine for women. What this image avoids is the fierce political rebellion inherent in demanding equal voice with male authors and the incredible tenacity of the volunteers who brought CALYX Journal to the page. While other small presses have withered away or been eaten up by corporate giants. CALYX's commitment to publishing the finest art and literature by women remains unswayed and just as necessary as it was forty years ago.

Perhaps it's lucky the early editors and volunteers didn't know what they were up against as an unfunded journal so far from the literati world of New York. They thought they would be in business for five years or so—the momentum of the women's movement was such that they, in their youthful zeal, assumed there would be no need for such a specialist press by the early 1980s. So they cut, typeset, and assembled the signatures, distributed journals, and camped at beach parks on their way to book fairs throughout the next decade.

Focusing on its collective editorial model, CALYX gained a reputation for innovation and diversity; to this day, the editors sit down together to argue for their favorites and make final selections. CALYX Journal published several themed issues as patterns began to emerge in submissions; this also provided opportunities to reach out to underserved communities and broaden the scope of material. The International Edition (1980) featured pieces both in their original language and in translation, including the first English translation of Wislawa Szymborska, who went on to win the Nobel Prize for Literature in 1986; the edition also presented the color prints of Frida Kahlo for the first time in the United States.

The late 1980s and early 1990s were prolific times for CALYX, particularly with the addition of CALYX Books in 1986. Between Bearing Witness/Sobreviviendo: AnAnthology of Writing and Art by Native American/ Latina Women and Women and Aging (both published in 1986), to a National Book Award for The Forbidden Stitch: An Asian American Women's Anthology in 1990, the journal was selling thousands of copies. But as chain bookstores and internet bookselling devoured independent bookstores and distributors, CALYX was forced to streamline and re-evaluate. Enter Into the Forest, Jean Hegland's dystopic novel of two sisters surviving infrastructural and social collapse: sold by hand to independent booksellers, the story traveled by word of mouth to New York and around the world and was reprinted in fourteen countries. A small-press bestselling fairy tale, Into the Forest enabled CALYX to flourish over the next decade and continues to bring in royalties—it was adapted for film in 2015.

Surviving the internet age has meant scaling back and scaling down; as ever, CALYX holds fast to the ideals of collective decision making, nurturing underrepresented voices, and producing high quality and beautiful materials against the grain of a publishing industry that seems to have no room for the careful and considered. CALYX's "before they were famous" list is filled with lauded international authors; it's impossible to know who on their pages today will be changing the literary world fifty years from now, but they will continue steadfastly nurturing and protecting the voices of the next generation.